500 FELT OBJECTS

500 FELT OBJECTS

CONTEMPORARY EXPLORATIONS OF A REMARKABLE MATERIAL

An Imprint of Sterling Publishing Co., Inc.
New York

WWW.LARKCRAFTS.COM

DEVELOPMENT EDITOR
Nathalie Mornu

EDITOR
Julie Hale

EDITORIAL ASSISTANCE
Dawn Dillingham, Abby Haffelt

ART DIRECTOR
Matt Shay

COVER DESIGNER
Matt Shay

FRONT COVER
Rosie Godbout
Tribal Manteau, 2008

BACK COVER, FROM LEFT
Aurelie Tu
Audrey LE Vessels: Large and Medium, 2010
(For alternate view, see p. 371)

Maricha Genovese
Under Pressure, 2009

Laura Kochevar
Flamenco Scarf, 2010

FRONT FLAP
Lothar Windels
Joseph Felt Chair, 2000

SPINE
Lisa Klakulak
Framed, 2009

BACK FLAP
Caroline Kelley
Ruffle Vase #1, 2007

TITLE PAGE
Anna Gunnasdòttir
Birth, 2007

OPPOSITE
Katelyn Aslett
Origami Wrap and *Rosie's Skirt*, 2006

Library of Congress Cataloging-in-Publication Data

Mornu, Nathalie.
  500 felt objects : contemporary explorations of a remarkable material /
[Nathalie Mornu, author]. -- 1st ed.
    p. cm.
  Includes index.
  ISBN 978-1-60059-705-3 (pb with flaps : alk. paper)
  1. Felt work. I. Title. II. Title: Five hundred felt objects.
  NK8899.5.W65A15 2011
  746'.0463--dc22
                                    2010051846
  10 9 8 7 6 5 4 3 2 1

First Edition

Published by Lark Crafts
An Imprint of Sterling Publishing Co., Inc.
387 Park Avenue South, New York, NY 10016

Text © 2011, Lark Crafts, an Imprint of Sterling Publishing Co., Inc.
Photography © 2011, Artist/Photographer

Distributed in Canada by Sterling Publishing,
c/o Canadian Manda Group, 165 Dufferin Street
Toronto, Ontario, Canada M6K 3H6

Distributed in the United Kingdom by GMC Distribution Services,
Castle Place, 166 High Street, Lewes, East Sussex, England BN7 1XU

Distributed in Australia by Capricorn Link (Australia) Pty Ltd.,
P.O. Box 704, Windsor, NSW 2756 Australia

If you have questions or comments about this book, please contact:
Lark Crafts, 67 Broadway, Asheville, NC 28801
828-253-0467

Manufactured in China

ISBN 13: 978-1-60059-705-3

For information about custom editions, special sales, premium, and corporate purchases, please contact the Sterling Special Sales Department at 800-805-5489 or specialsales@sterlingpub.com.

For information about desk and examination copies available to college and university professors, submit requests to academic@larkbooks.com.
Our complete policy can be found at www.larkcrafts.com.

Contents

Introduction

Felt making as a creative discipline is taking shape before our eyes.

Once relegated to the areas of heavy industry and children's crafts, felt now plays a complex role in designs of all kinds. From jewelry and furniture to clothing and decorative art, the material accommodates a range of moods, aesthetic styles, and purposes.

Traditional art mediums like ceramics and woodworking have benefitted from hundreds of years of refinement by highly skilled practitioners. With felt, that process is happening now. New techniques are being developed in studios and shared in workshops around the world. Felt artists are innovating like mad. As you'll discover when you peruse these pages, today's designers employ a variety of techniques, including traditional wet felting, hybrid felting, and needle felting. They use felt that's made by hand and by machine. Through work that's remarkably eclectic, they're demonstrating how, over the past few decades, the material's identity has changed.

Felt has been in use across Central Asia for thousands of years. Believed to be one of the earliest man-made materials, it arose during the Neolithic period and was indispensable to nomadic cultures like the Mongols, who used it to make items as varied and necessary as saddles, boots, body armor, and circular tents called yurts. Among nomadic cultures, felt was also worked into colorfully patterned carpets, tent bands, bags, and clothing. Many of the artists in this book reference these societies in their work. Bita Ghezelayagh's *Felt Memories III* beautifully evokes the material's ties to traditional cultures.

It wasn't until the 1970s that artists outside the traditional felt-making societies began investigating felt as both a creative medium and a rich vein of scholarly study.

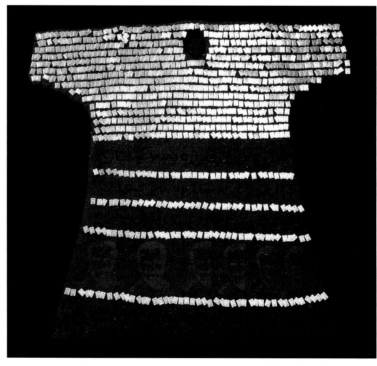

Bita Ghezelayagh
Felt Memories III | 2009

Exposure to the felts of nomadic peoples through exhibitions and books such as M. E. Burkett's *Art of the Felt Maker* catalyzed a period of intensive field research from North Africa to Mongolia. Inspired experimentation also took place in the studios of artists, who loved the unique physicality of the material.

In western Europe and the Americas, felt has typically been valued for technical rather than aesthetic reasons. Self-extinguishing, capable of holding large amounts of fluid without feeling wet, and sound-absorbing, felt has long been ubiquitous but invisible—a gray part of the industrial landscape.

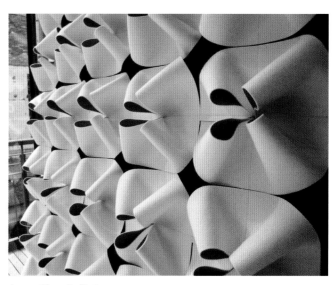

Anne Kyyrö Quinn
Rosette Acoustic Wall Panel | 2006

Kathryn Walter
FELT Striation: Screening Room Doors | 2006

Today, however, it's front and center in the worlds of architecture and design. Large-scale architectural installations now showcase the material's unique ability to temper the acoustic environment while creating a dramatic visual surface. In this book, pieces like Anne Kyyrö Quinn's *Rosette Acoustic Wall Panel* and Kathryn Walter's *Screening Room Doors* use felt as an architectural component—an element that provides practical support while beautifully enhancing a room's mood.

Without a doubt, crafters are stretching the boundaries of the felt making discipline. Taking advantage of wool's natural tendency to shrink and entangle, many artists actually felt through a variety of fabrics, including silk, gauze, lace, and velvet, to completely change the look and feel of the material and create a wide variety of surface textures. In this book, you'll find pieces that synthesize a range of materials. Jorie Johnson's *Flare Coat* is a mix of merino and silk organza that has a wonderfully delicate finish. Janice Arnold's substantial, sumptuous *Necklett* (page 150) combines merino fleece, silk, and velvet. Both pieces demonstrate felt's potential to be transformed through a rich blend of fabrics.

Jorie Johnson
Sumi Series: Flare Coat | 2008

Other designers take a sculptural approach, molding the material, which can be made thin and flexible or dense and hard, into three-dimensional forms. Two very different pieces, VANDERBOS' elegantly contoured *embracement #036* and Stephanie Metz's striking *Teddy Skull: Ursulus disneyus solicitudo*, demonstrate the range of forms and effects that can be achieved.

Perhaps because of the immediacy of the felting process, the material brings to mind a natural or raw substance. Inspired by this quality, many contemporary artists are creating pieces that mimic plants or organic matter—everything from stones to seaweed. Elis Vermeulen's *Barnacles* (page 257), Marjolein Dallinga's *Red Craters*, and Jodi Colella's *Seeds* (page 263) skillfully exploit felt's natural, unrefined side. These pieces are artful yet a little bit wild, with the exoticism of strange specimens found in nature.

Industrial felt is featured in many of this book's selections. Since Joseph Beuys' experiments with the heavyduty material in the 1960s, it has been consistently

VANDERBOS
embracement #036 | 2004

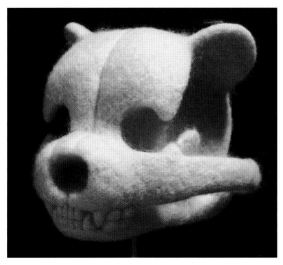

Stephanie Metz
Teddy Skull: Ursulus disneyus solicitudo | 2008

influential in the art world. The popularity of repurposing and recycling has brought it fresh attention from designers. On these pages, you'll find Kathryn Walter's gorgeous quilts and wall coverings, which feature industrial felt remnants, and wearable pieces like Lilyana Bekic's *Grey Corollarium* that employ the material in sophisticated ways.

Lilyana Bekic
Grey Corollarium | 2009

Marjolein Dallinga
Red Craters | 2009

With contributions by crafters from around the world, this volume is a testament to felt's international appeal. I'd like to acknowledge with appreciation all of the designers who participated and to thank Lark Crafts for giving me the opportunity to serve as juror for the project. The artists featured here use felt in ways that were unimaginable 40 years ago. Their creations range from playful to elegant to practical, making this a collection that celebrates the full diversity of what felt is now. I hope you enjoy it.

Susan Brown

Catherine O'Leary
Untitled | 2009
88 X 65 CM
Merino wool fleece, silk; wet felted,
nuno techniques, stitched
PHOTO BY ARTIST

VANDERBOS

embracement #058 | 2007

65 X 50 X 25 CM

Industrial felt; sewn, steam molded

PHOTO BY MIRJAM VERSCHOOR

Hut Up
Jacket J 22 and *Skirt KWS 9/4* | 2010
DIMENSIONS VARY
Merino wool, cotton, silk
DESIGNED BY CHRISTINE BIRKLE
PHOTO BY ARTIST

Lara Grant
Arched Coatdress | 2007
114.3 CM LONG

Merino fleece, polyester thread, covered buttons;
wet felted, needle felted, sewn, blocked

ANKLE ACCESSORIES DESIGNED BY CHRYSTIE CAPPELLI
PHOTOS BY ARUN NEVADER

Ulrieke Benner
Coat of Many Colors | 2008
91.1 CM LONG
Merino wool, silk; wet felted, nuno techniques
PHOTO BY JOHN CAMERON

Gar Wang
Watermelon Hat | 2003
50.8 X 25.4 CM
Merino wool; wet felted
PHOTO BY CLAUS WICKRATH

Leiko Uchiyama

Mosaic | 2009

160 X 50 CM

Merino wool, silk fabric;
dyed, wet felted

PHOTO BY KAZUHIRO KOBUSHI

Sue Heathcote
Wrap | 2006
184 X 28 CM
Lamb's wool; machine knitted,
hand manipulated
PHOTOS BY NOEL SHELLEY

Katelyn Aslett
Origami Wrap and *Rosie's Skirt* | 2006
WRAP: 63 X 120 CM; SKIRT: 65 X 145 CM
Merino, silk; hand dyed, hand felted
PHOTOS BY ROSIE KERSCH

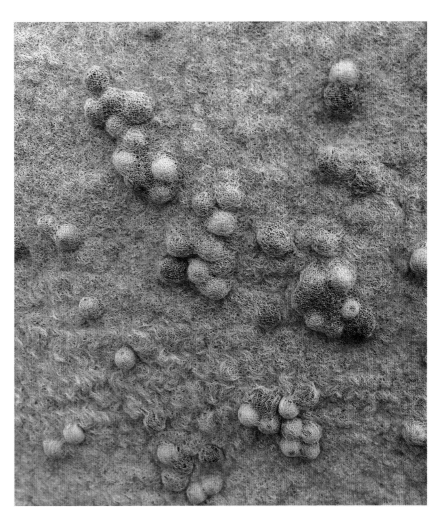

Anneke Copier

Sheba | 2007

135 CM LONG

Wool, silk, peppercorns; wet felted

PHOTOS BY ARTIST

Hut Up

Top KST 9/5 and *Skirt KSS 6/3* | 2010

DIMENSIONS VARY

Merino wool, silk

DESIGNED BY CHRISTINE BIRKLE
PHOTO BY ARTIST

Anneke Copier

Elsas | 2010

145 CM LONG

Silk, flax, wool; nuno techniques, wet felted

PHOTO BY ARTIST

Katie Coble

Mirrored Felt Piece Folded | 2009

82 X 30 X 15 CM

Industrial felt, linen thread, polyester, elastic; cut, stitched, sewn

PHOTO BY TOM FOLEY

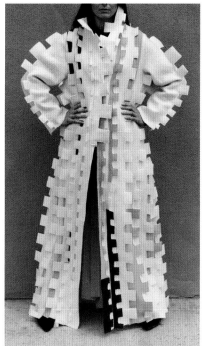

Maggy Pavlou
Armadillo Coat | 2009
57 CM LONG
Merino fleece; wet felted, pieced, stitched
PHOTOS BY KEVIN FACER

Carol Ingram

Marketplace Wrap | 2009

172.7 X 36.8 CM

Merino roving, commercial merino pre-felt, paj silk, rayon, silk chiffon; hand dyed, wet felted, nuno techniques

PHOTO BY JODY BREWER

Rosie Godbout

Perfecto Vest | 2007

80 X 43 CM

Merino fleece, silk, rayon; wet felted

PHOTO BY DAVID BISHOP NORIEGA

Yohji Yamamoto
Stylized Sculpture 001 | 2007
DIMENSIONS NOT AVAILABLE
Felt
PHOTO BY SUGIMOTO STUDIO
COURTESY OF KYOTO COSTUME INSTITUTE

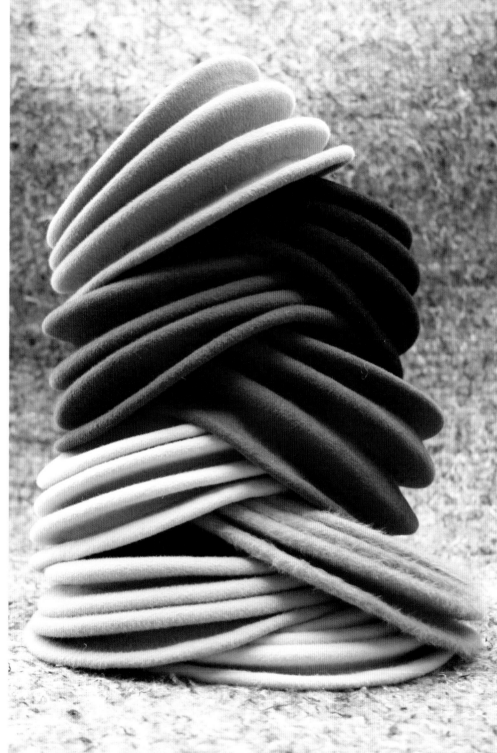

Waltraud Reiner
Travel Hats | 1993
EACH: 20 X 17 CM
Industrial felt; blocked
PHOTO BY ARTIST

Vidàk Istvàn

Shibori Woman | 2004

160 X 45 CM

Merino fleece; indigo dyed, shibori, wet felted

PHOTO BY ÀGH ANDRAS

Lyn Pflueger

ruana | 2007

127 X 110 CM

Merino fleece, yak and silk fibers, silk
chiffon fabric; dyed, nuno techniques

PHOTO BY JOANNE HAMEL

Uta Marschmann
Adire Eleko: Path to the Mill | 2007
160 X 50 CM
Merino fleece, natural indigo; wet felted,
dyed, reserve technique
PHOTO BY ALEXANDER HEUBERGER

Sheila Ahern
Cloche Hat | 2008
16 X 25 CM
Merino fleece, mulberry silk; wet felted
PHOTO BY JOANNA TOMASZEWSKA

Horst
Deadwood | 2009
150 X 120 X 120 CM
Falkland wool; wet felted, dyed
PHOTO BY ARTIST

I live on the Russian border in North Karelia, Finland, and have been exploring Karelian folk embroidery for some time now. It was the main inspiration for this design. The hat was completely wet felted in a single piece; there's no needlework or needle felting in it whatsoever. —KA

Karoliina Arvilommi
Karelia Hat | 2007
35 X 35 X 20 CM
Finnish Landrace wool batting, yarn; wet felted
PHOTO BY LISELOTTE HABETS

Jorie Johnson

First Snow Series: Long Coat | 2006

125 X 65 X 30 CM

Swiss Walliser fleece, polyester fluorescent fiber,
knitting yarn; hand felted, seamless technique

PHOTO BY YOU KOBAYASHI

Hut Up

Jacket with Frills J 10 and *Flared Skirt KWS 10/11* | 2010

DIMENSIONS VARY

Merino wool, cotton

DESIGNED BY CHRISTINE BIRKLE
PHOTO BY ARTIST

Miriam Carter
Asian Vest with Slash Scarf | 2009
DIMENSIONS NOT AVAILABLE
Merino fleece, silk organza, cotton;
nuno techniques
PHOTO BY GYAKYI BONSU-ANANE

Bottura Sabrina
Column Hat | 2009
19 X 17 X 18 CM
Merino fleece; wet felted, handmade
PHOTO BY ARTIST

À La Disposition
Molded Jacket Fall and Winter | 2008
76.2 X 50.8 X 22.8 CM
Felt; blocked, stitched
PHOTO BY ARTIST

These pieces explore the sculptural potential of felt, particularly wet felt's ability to be molded and retain its shape when dry. The perforations in the shirt weren't cut. They resulted from the careful placement of merino and silk fibers, which also gave the edges of the shirt a soft, undulating look. —GW

Gar Wang
Broccoli Crown and *Hole-Y Shirt* | 2003
CROWN: 30 X 23 CM; SHIRT: 50 X 50 CM
Silk, merino wool; hand dyed, felted
PHOTO BY CLAUS WICKRATH

Anne Sheikh

The Life Aquatic | 1995

132 X 60.9 CM

Silk chiffon, silk charmeuse, angora and merino fleece, abalone button; needle felted, wet felted, hand dyed, sewn

PHOTOS BY JOHN E. BAER

This garment was inspired by Botticelli's The Birth of Venus. *As I experimented with felting, I discovered that my favorite part of the finished product was always the edges—wonderfully organic and irregular, as in this piece.* —AS

Gina Gomba
Gigli Jacket | 2009
67 X 51 X 0.2 CM
Merino fleece, silk chiffon; wet
felted, dyed, nuno techniques
PHOTO BY ARTIST

Eibhilín Mhic Fhearraigh
Sweep Everyday | 2009
15 X 27 X 23 CM
Peach bloom felt; blocked, hand molded
PHOTO BY RICHARD COSTELLOE

Hut Up

Jacket KWJ 9/1 and *Skirt KWS 9/3* | 2010

DIMENSIONS VARY

Merino wool, cotton, silk

DESIGNED BY CHRISTINE BIRKLE
PHOTO BY ARTIST

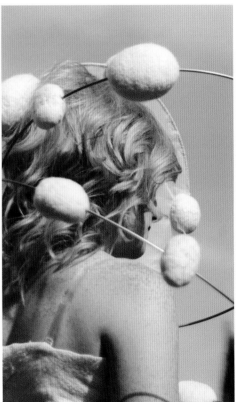

Marian Kastelein

Circles in the Sky | 2009

DIMENSIONS NOT AVAILABLE

Merino wool, silk, linen, flax; wet felted

PHOTOS BY MARIA DOELMAN

Sharit by Charity vd Meer Musoma

Stormy Weather | 2009

SIZE 38

Wool, silk; nuno techniques

PHOTO BY HARRY TIELMAN

Joo Hee
Folding Slippers | 2009
EACH: 28 X 11 X 0.3 CM
Melan felt, hard felt, snap fastener; stitched, glued
PHOTO BY ARTIST

Tupu Mentu
Untitled | 2009
2 X 25 X 16 CM
Merino fleece, silk; wet felted,
dyed, stitched, steamed
PHOTO BY SAKARI MENTU

Lene Frantzen
Scarf | 2000
90 X 200 CM
Wool, silk; wet felted
PHOTO BY THOMAS GUNGE

VANDERBOS
embracement #036 | 2004
83 X 50 X 25 CM
Industrial felt; sewn, steam molded
PHOTOS BY JAN BOEVE AMSTERDAM

À La Disposition

Pannier Jacket Fall and Winter | 2009

91.4 X 68.5 X 45.7 CM

Felt; blocked, stitched

PHOTO BY ARTIST

Leiko Uchiyama

Bolero | 2009

40 X 125 CM

Merino wool, silk fiber; dyed, wet felted

PHOTO BY KAZUHIRO KOBUSHI

Yvonne Wakabayashi
Black Hand-Cut Wool Lace Shrug | 2009
DIMENSIONS NOT AVAILABLE
Single-knit wool; cut, wet felted,
clamped, dyed, stitched, blocked
PHOTOS BY KENJI NAGAI

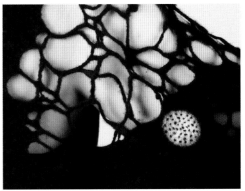

Jean Hicks
Sushi Hat | 1999
17.8 X 17.8 CM
Merino, silk, wood; hand felted,
traditional millinery techniques
PHOTO BY JAN COOK

Gioia Danielis
Reversible Jacket | 2009
73 X 49 X 0.3 CM
Merino fleece, Bergschaf fleece, silk,
silk chiffon; wet felted, dyed, nuno techniques
PHOTO BY ARTIST

Jorie Johnson

Sumi Series: Flare Coat | 2008

84 X 98 X 5 CM

Merino pre-felt, silk organza, silk fibers, pencil roving, metal and lacquer buttons; sumi painted, clamp resisted, de-gummed, hand felted seamless construction

PHOTOS BY YOU KOBAYASHI

Jean Hicks

Brimmed Corazon | 2009

33 X 27.9 CM

Merino wool, cashmere, alpaca; hand felted, traditional millinery techniques

PHOTO BY JAN COOK

Anneke Copier

Hindeloopen | 2009

150 CM LONG

Wool, flax; wet felted

PHOTO BY ARTIST

Lone Åsbjerg
Top | 2008
70 X 50 CM
Gauze, silk fibers, fine merino wool; nuno techniques
PHOTO BY ARTIST

Latifa Medjdoub

Lioness | 2008

127 X 61 X 38 CM

Merino wool; knitted, fulled, felted

PHOTOS BY ARTIST

Cheryl Kamera
Untitled | 2008
56 X 150 CM
Silk mesh chiffon, merino fleece, devoré
velvet; wet felted, dyed, nuno techniques
PHOTO BY MICHAEL STADLER

Jessica De Haas
Untitled | 2009
50 X 37 X 24 CM
Merino fleece, silk fabric, cotton thread, seed
beads, millenary tulle; wet felted, dyed, stitched
PHOTO BY SHIMON KARMEL

Teresa Byström
Le Style ou l'Art Nouilles
(The Noodle Style or Art Nouveau) | 2009
158.8 X 20.3 CM

Merino fleece, tussah silk top, bombyx silk top,
throwster's waste, silk gauze, silk/rayon velvet,
Czechoslovakian glass button; wet felted, dyed, silk-
screened, devoré process, nuno techniques, blocked

PHOTO BY JAMES HART STUDIO

Tammy L. Deck

Sea-Green Shawl | 2009

101.6 X 101.6 CM

Merino cross fleece, silk gauze, wool, mohair, metallic
yarns; hand dyed, wet felted, nuno techniques

PHOTO BY ARTIST

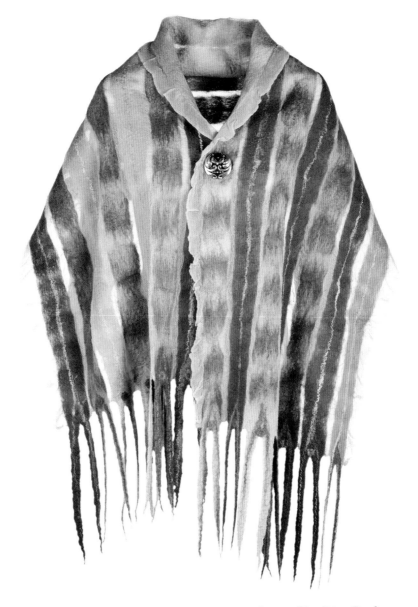

Lone Birgitte Carlsen

Ikat | 2006

200 X 47 CM

Wool, silk fabric, silk fibers; wet felted, nuno techniques

PHOTO BY JEPPE CARLSEN

Vilte Kazlauskaite

Wild Pigeon | 2009

109.2 CM LONG

Merino wool, silk chiffon, raw silk; nuno
techniques, dyed, stamped with plants

PHOTO BY ARTIST

Rowena Choi
Branché | 2006
46 X 36 X 5 CM
Industrial wool felt, steel wire; stitched

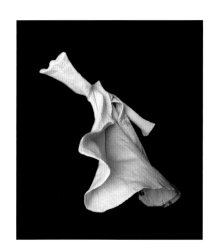

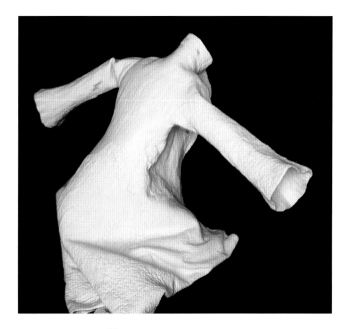

Françoise Hoffmann

Au Large de Cape Ann | 2010

DIMENSIONS UNAVAILABLE

Merino wool, silk georgette; digitally printed

PHOTOS BY ALDO PAREDES

Maggie Scott

From the Matchstick Collection: Turquoise Shawl | 2009

250 X 70 CM

Merino wool, silk fiber; hand felted, nuno technique

PHOTO BY LAURENT MOULIN

Anna-Katherine Curfman
Swirls | 2009
203.2 X 45.7 CM
Merino roving, silk organza; nuno techniques, wet felted
PHOTO BY ARTIST

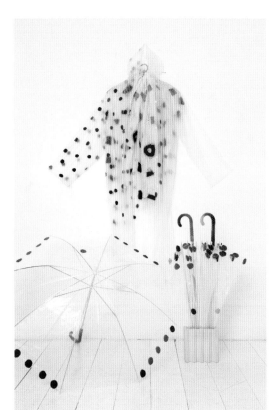

Jorie Johnson
Weather Report: Slicker and Snow Umbrellas | 2008
DIMENSIONS VARY
Merino and crossbreed fleece, vinyl, silk mesh shawls;
needle punched, wet felted
PHOTOS BY YUZO TOYODA

Eia Radosavljevic
Colimaçon | 1991
17 X 20 X 20 CM
Industrial felt, cotton thread,
cotton/rayon grosgrain, wire,
elastic; machine sewn, hand stitched
PHOTO BY ARTIST

Ulrieke Benner

Wonderland | 2008

213.4 X 86.4 CM

Merino wool, silk fabrics; nuno collage, wet felted

PHOTOS BY JOHN CAMERON

Cristina Garcia
Forest Jacket | 2009
SIZE 10
Silk, fleece; nuno techniques
PHOTOS BY JOANNA TOMASZEWSKA

Lisa Klakulak
Bound Buttons Shawl | 2005
162.6 X 40.6 CM
Merino and Finn/Rambouillet wool fleece, silk
fabric, wooden buttons; wet felted, naturally
dyed with cochineal insects and indigo
PHOTO BY JOHN LUCAS

Cathryn Ward
Felt and Muslin Wrap | 2009
150 X 40 CM
Merino fleece, muslin; wet
felted, nuno techniques
PHOTOS BY JOLENE CARTMILL

Tupu Mentu
Wedding Dress | 2005
SIZE 8
Merino fleece, cotton; wet felted,
stitched, steamed, sewn
PHOTO BY JULIANA HARKKI

Kirsti Ravnå Tverå
Eugenia | 2007
56 CM
Merino wool; nuno techniques
PHOTO BY ANNE KARI MYRVIK

Tash Wesp
Coat of Blues | 2009
28 X 217 CM
Merino fleece, cotton, rayon, silk fabrics;
wet felted, seamless nuno, hand dyed
PHOTO BY THOMAS OSBORNE

Rosie Godbout
Tribal Manteau | 2008
105 X 45 CM
Merino fleece, Indian
cotton; nuno techniques
PHOTO BY DAVID BISHOP NORIEGA

Grazia Galli
Laura Salvioni
Notte/Twilight | 2008
SIZE 8
Merino, cotton gauze; nuno techniques
PHOTOS BY DAVIDE CERATI

Beth Andrews

Untitled | 2009

81 X 44 CM

Merino fleece, wood button, industrial steel pieces;
wet felted, resist, tailored, needle punched, resist dyed

PHOTOS BY ARTIST

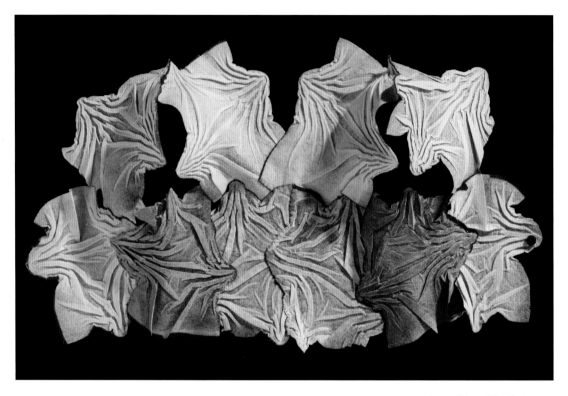

Leaf Vest *is part of a series that may be worn or placed on the wall. Each piece in the series employs different manipulations to create a variety of textures and to express the metaphors present in nature.* —ALH

Ana Lisa Hedstrom
Leaf Vest | 2008
50 X 96 CM
Synthetic felt; hand stitched, manipulated, dye sublimation transfer printed
PHOTO BY DON TUTTLE

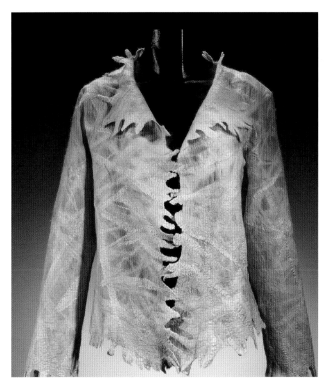

Miriam Carter

Laminated Sheer Jacket | 2008

DIMENSIONS NOT AVAILABLE

Merino wool, silk; nuno techniques, hand dyed

PHOTO BY RALPH GABRINER

Susan J. Bowman

Canyon Stone | 2010

63 X 134 X 2 CM

Merino yarn, silk, acid dyes, vat
dyes; woven, shibori, felted, sewn

PHOTO BY SARA CRANDALL

Dena J. Gershon

Bering Strait Vest | 2008

58.4 X 52 X 36 CM

Merino wool and fleece, silk
fibers; wet felted, hand dyed

PHOTOS BY ROBERT BANKS

When I work with felt, I try to be innovative and exploit the material's creative potential. It's a versatile medium that offers extraordinary design potential. Created from handcrafted felt, Boa is my personal response to the dramatic feathered accessory. —LC

Liz Clay
Boa | 2003
185 X 30 CM
Merino wool, cashmere, silk, chiffon; wet felted
PHOTO BY CLIVE BOURSNELL

Pam de Groot

Rainbow Wrap | 2009

170 X 60 CM

Australian merino wool, recycled silk fabric, synthetic fabric, wooden ring and spike; wet felted, nuno techniques

PHOTO BY ARTIST

Mollie Littlejohn

Floating Wool | 2005

65 CM LONG

Merino fleece, silk gauze, silk waste; dyed, pieced, hand stitched, nuno techniques

PHOTO BY ARTIST

Laura Kochevar

Flamenco Wrap | 2010

157.5 X 40.6 CM

Merino, silk chiffon; nuno techniques, stretched

PHOTO BY ARTIST

Michela Gregoretti (Tinakela)

Nine Steps Inwards | 2010

30 X 28 CM

Merino wool; wet felted

PHOTO BY URBAN GOLOB

VANDERBOS
embracement #059 | 2007
60 X 45 X 25 CM
Industrial felt; sewn, steam molded
PHOTOS BY MIRJAM VERSCHOOR

**Elisabeth Berthon for
Lola Bastille-Paris**

Flower Coat | 2010

133 X 93 X 40 CM

Merino fleece, mohair, Wensleydale
wool, cotton gauze; wet felted

PHOTO BY CHLOE LECOUP

Valya

Apron Vignette | 2010

107 X 137 CM

Merino fleece, silk gauze; hand painted, wet felted

PHOTO BY ARTIST

Hut Up
Jacket KWJ 10/3 and
Flared Skirt KWS 10/7 | 2010
DIMENSIONS VARY
Merino wool, cotton
DESIGNED BY CHRISTINE BIRKLE
PHOTO BY ARTIST

Jean Hicks

Spiral Two-Part Brim | 2009

30.4 X 22.8 CM

Alpaca merino, Norwegian wool; hand felted, traditional
millinery techniques

PHOTO BY JAN COOK

Anastasia Bespalova
Pumpkin Baby Hat | 2009
20 X 15 CM
Merino wool, merino and mohair blend; wet felted
PHOTOS BY ARTIST

Lone Åsbjerg
Poncho | 2009
110 X 100 CM
Silk fibers, flax, fine merino wool; nuno techniques
PHOTOS BY ARTIST

Torill Haugsvær Wilberg
Winter Bride | 2009
150 X 66 X 50 CM
Silk georgette, merino wool, lace;
hand felted, nuno techniques
PHOTO BY TORBJGRN TANDBERG

Jean Williams Cacicedo
Rain Coat: S.F. Bay | 1999
132.1 X 127 CM
Wool; felted, dyed, pieced, punched, sewn
PHOTO BY BARRY SHAPIRO

Pam de Groot

Armadillo Hat | 2009

25 X 25 CM

Australian merino wool, recycled
silk fabric; wet felted, blocked

PHOTO BY ARTIST

Gioia Danielis

Reversible Jacket | 2009

73 X 49 X 0.3 CM

Merino fleece, Bergschaf fleece, silk,
silk chiffon; wet felted, dyed, nuno techniques

PHOTO BY ARTIST

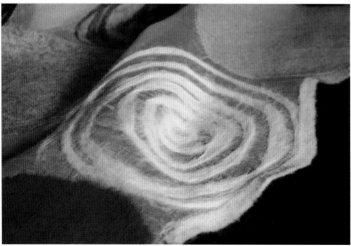

Elena Kihlman

Dots Runner | 2008

180 X 60 CM

Merino wool, silk organza; felted, nuno techniques

PHOTOS BY ELEONORA BLANCO

Anna-Katherine Curfman
Circumference | 2008
188 X 45.7 CM
Merino roving, iridescent silk chiffon;
nuno techniques, wet felted
PHOTO BY DAVID EMERY

Yvonne Wakabayashi

Chartreuse Nui Shibori Lace Shawl | 2008

56 X 148 CM

Single-knit wool jersey; dyed, shibori, cut, slashed, wet felted, blocked

PHOTOS BY KENJI NAGAI

As a Canadian with a Japanese background, I create work with layers of meaning, fusing Eastern and Western aesthetics, the traditional and the contemporary. Felt is a material that allows me to play up the idea of multiple dimensions, textures, and layers. —YW

Claudia Moeller
Posh Wool: Wraparound Top and *Sarouel Pants* | 2007
SIZE 10

Pure silk crêpe georgette, Australian merino wool,
silk fibers, vintage lace patches, silk organza,
embroidered ribbons; wet felted, nuno techniques

PHOTO BY ARTIST

Tiina Mikkelä
Kesäheinä Evening Dress | 2006
DIMENSIONS NOT AVAILABLE
Merino wool, cotton fabrics; wet felted, stitched
PHOTOS BY JULIANA HARKKI

Anna-Katherine Curfman

Butterfly Fairy | 2009

50.8 X 30.5 X 10.2 CM

Merino pre-felt, merino roving, silk chiffon, silk;
stitched, nuno techniques, wet felted

PHOTOS BY ARTIST

Katie Coble

Right Felt Form Unfolded into a Ruff | 2009

91 X 61 X 40 CM

Industrial felt, linen thread, wool, satin, string; cut, stitched, sewn

PHOTO BY TOM FOLEY

Phyllis Beals
Pinwheel | 1999
14 X 23 X 22 CM
Fur felt, vintage button; hand
blocked, sculpted, appliquéd
PHOTO BY ARTIST

Ulrieke Benner
Tango Passion | 2009
71.1 CM LONG
Wool, silk; shibori, stitched, felted, tailored
PHOTO BY JOHN CAMERON

Maria Winner
Double Up | 2007
32 X 222 CM
Merino wool yarn, metallic thread; hand-woven
interlaced double weave technique, wet felted
PHOTO BY JOHN TELFORD

Grazia Galli
Laura Salvioni
Abbraccio/Hold Me | 2008
SIZE 8
Merino, cotton gauze; nuno techniques
PHOTOS BY DAVIDE CERATI

Yvonne Wakabayashi
Grey Nui Shibori Jacket | 2008
101.6 CM LONG
Single-knit jersey; shibori, wet felted, blocked
PHOTOS BY KENJI NAGAI

Kirsti Ravnå Tverå
Ingela | 2007
56 CM
Merino wool; nuno techniques
PHOTO BY ANNE KARI MYRVIK

Beth Andrews
Untitled | 2009

76 X 48 CM

Merino fleece, upcycled silk, cotton thread, belt,
industrial steel pieces; wet felted using resist,
attached, resist dyed, nuno techniques, cut

PHOTOS BY ARTIST

Pam de Groot
Bush Priestess Gown and Hat | 2009

HAT: 80 X 80 CM; GOWN: SIZE 10-12

Merino wool, silk fabric, muslin cloth, silk top, beads, shells, seed pods; wet felted, eco dyed and printed, embroidered, stitched

PHOTO BY ARTIST

Liz Clay

Untitled | 2008

140 X 90 CM

Merino fleece; wet felted, hand
dyed, inlaid, hand stitched

DESIGNED BY STELLA MCCARTNEY
PHOTO BY GUCCI

Jessica De Haas
Au Natural | 2008

102 X 45 X 30 CM

Merino fleece, silk fabric, thread, button;
wet felted, pre-felt techniques, stitched

PHOTO BY NENAD STEVANOVIC

Anna-Katherine Curfman
Newsprint | 2009

183 X 55.9 CM

Merino pre-felt, merino roving, silk
chiffon; nuno techniques, wet felted

PHOTO BY ARTIST

Lilyana Bekic

Grey Corollarium | 2009

21.6 X 53.3 X 6.4 CM

Fur felt, silk cocoons; partially hand dyed,
blocked, hand formed, hand stitched

PHOTOS BY ARTIST

With fur felt, I'm able to create large neckpieces that are incredibly light and sculptural. Traditionally used in millinery, the material takes on a new life in these ornamental pieces. —LB

Christina A. Hogan

Asclepius Collar | 2008

20.5 X 20.5 X 10 CM

Peruvian highland wool yarn, milkweed pods, glass beads, sterling silver, patina; knitted, fulled, twined, beaded, forged, soldered

PHOTO BY DAVID NEVALA

Michelle Miller
Fold Series Necklaces | 2009
DIMENSIONS VARY
Industrial felt, sterling silver, nylon-coated wire; constructed
PHOTO BY ARTIST

Sezgin Akan
Loop Collar | 2007
25 CM IN DIAMETER
Merino fleece, cord; dyed, wet felted, needle felted, stitched
PHOTO BY EVREN ARISOY

Laura Phillips
Untitled and *Quiet* | 2009
UNTITLED (LEFT): 5 X 8.2 X 7.6 CM; QUIET (RIGHT): 4 X 9.5 X 5.2 CM
Merino fleece, brass beads, silk thread, aluminum;
wet felted, resist dyed, folded, stitched, beaded
PHOTO BY AARON PADEN

Lisa Klakulak

Framed | 2009

30.5 X 25.4 X 11.5 CM

Merino and Finn/Rambouillet wool fleece, cotton and waxed linen thread, plastic tubing; wet felted, dyed, free-motion machine embroidered, hand stitched, steam blocked

PHOTOS BY STEVE MANN

Elizabeth Rubidge
Molly Scarf | 2008
163 CM LONG
Merino wool; wet felted, hand cut
PHOTO BY BARRETT KOWALSKY

Megan Auman
cozy/cuff | 2009
6.4 X 7.6 X 7.6 CM
Industrial wool felt, thread; laser cut, stitched
PHOTOS BY ARTIST

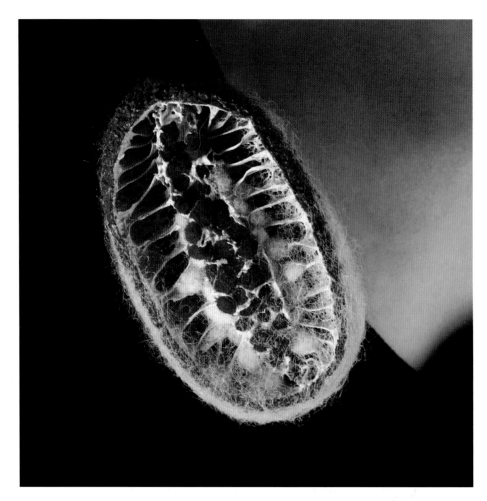

Eun Yeong Jeong
Segmented Life brooch | 2007
11 X 6.5 X 4 CM
Loofah, wool, sterling silver, plastic, stainless
steel; wet felted, needle felted, dyed, soldered
PHOTO BY ARTIST

Jennifer Moss
Reproduction II | 2008
56 X 16 X 5 CM
Merino wool, nylon, silk thread, pearls;
wet felted, needle felted, sewn
PHOTO BY ARTIST

Agostina Zwilling

feltrigami Shopper A | 2008

75 X 32 X 2 CM

Merino fleece, leather handles, silk
threads; wet felted, stitched

PHOTOS BY MARCO BRAVI

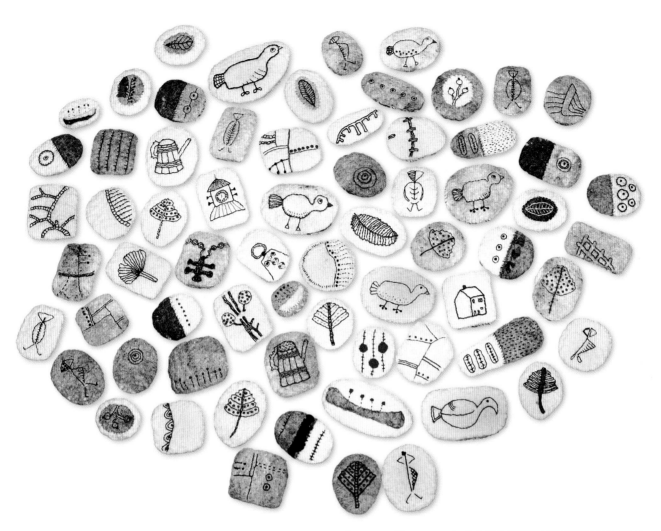

Inspired by a trip I made to Oslo, Norway, these brooches are hand-felted stitched drawings based on studies taken from archaeological finds, Viking ships, and historical artifacts. Felt was the ideal canvas for me to draw on with stitches. —JH

Joanne Haywood
Oslo Brooches | 2005
AVERAGE SIZE: 5 X 5 X 0.7 CM
Merino fleece, silver, cotton yarn; wet felted, embroidered, formed, soldered
PHOTOS BY ALAN PARKINSON

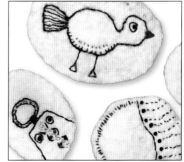

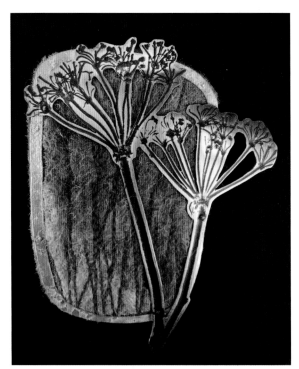

Cari-Jane Hakes
A Life without Love Is Like a Year without Summer | 2010
6 X 5.5 X 0.4 CM
Merino fleece, silver, copper, patina; wet felted,
machine stitched, roller printed, hand fabricated
PHOTO BY ARTIST

Lisa Klakulak
Untitled | 2007
EACH: 8.9 X 1.3 X 4.5 CM
Merino wool fleece, amber and glass seed beads, sterling
silver wire; wet felted, naturally dyed with Osage-orange
wood and madder root, hand stitched, beaded, forged
PHOTO BY STEVE MANN

Jane Cummins
Conference Bags | 2009
EACH: 36 X 26 X 10 CM
Merino fleece, birch plywood; wet felted
PHOTO BY WARD

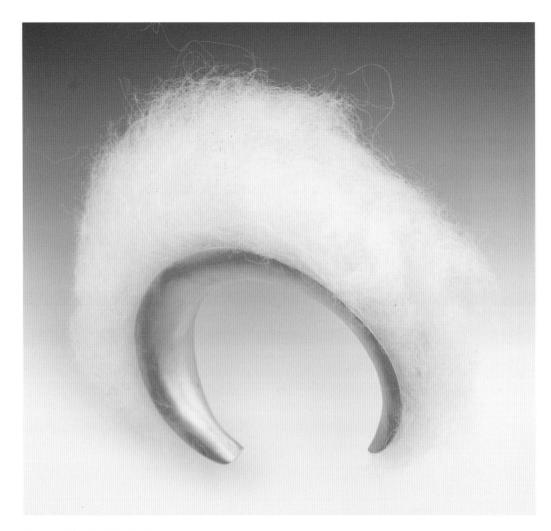

Kenneth C. MacBain
Felt Bracelet | 2010
10 X 10 X 4.5 CM
Wool felt, brass
PHOTO BY ARTIST

Hisano Takei

Stackable | 2006

LARGEST SECTION: 37 X 33.5 X 15 CM

Wool; needle felted, wet felted, starched

PHOTOS BY ROBERT STORM

Gräf & Lantz

Duffle Bag | 2009

35.6 X 45.7 X 19.1 CM

Merino felt, vegetable-tanned leather

PHOTO BY ARTIST

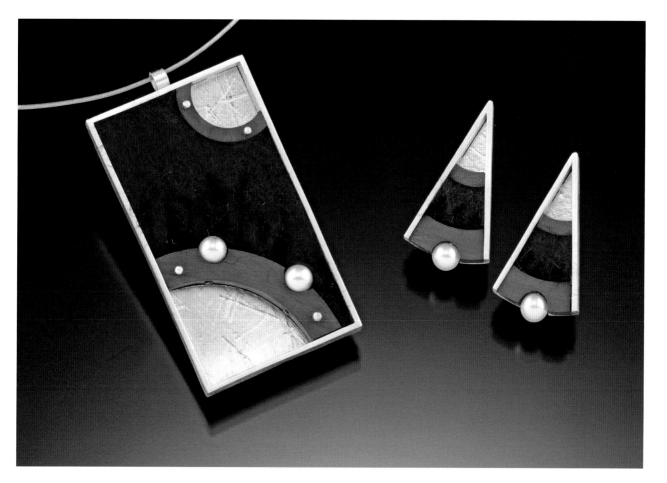

Thea Clark
Red Pendant and Earrings | 2007

PENDANT: 5 X 2.9 X 0.3 CM; EACH EARRING: 2.8 X 1.5 X 0.4 CM

Merino roving, silver, polyvinyl chloride, 22-karat gold bi-metal, pearls; wet felted, needle felted, formed, textured, soldered, riveted

PHOTO BY LARRY SANDERS

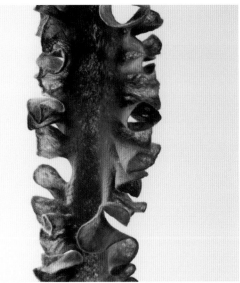

Tracy White

Untitled | 2009

120 X 15 X 4 CM

Merino wool, silk; dyed, wet felted

PHOTOS BY HELMUT HIRLER

My neckpieces feature a variety of three-dimensional surfaces based on structures found in nature. Felt, with its sculptural qualities, allows me to build up several layers in each piece, to mold, stretch, and condense until I have a seamless object. —DB

Dagmar Binder
Series of 3D Structured Neckpieces | 2006
EACH: 220 X 40 CM
Merino tops; wet felted
PHOTO BY ARTIST

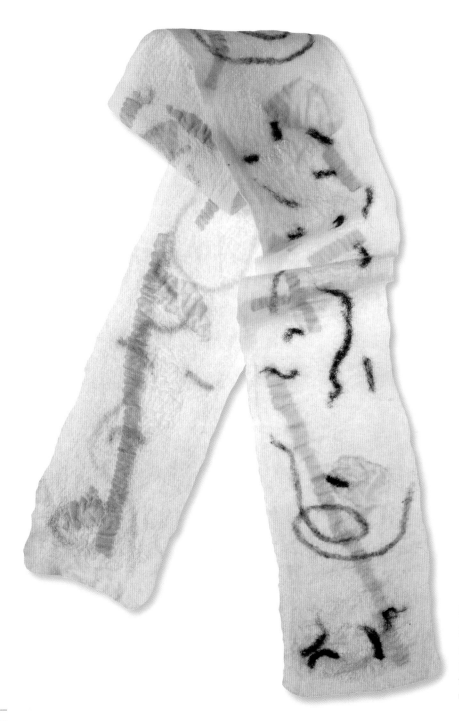

Robyn A. Daniel
Graffiti au Naturel Scarf | 2007
148.5 X 14 CM
Merino wool, silk, various fabrics;
wet felted, nuno technique
PHOTO BY JOHN POLAK

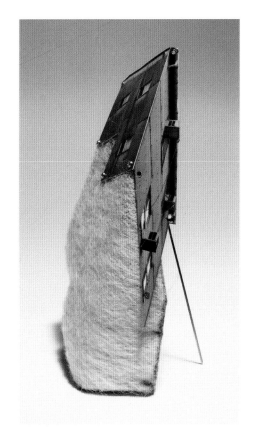

Yung-Huei Chao

Extension Series III: Brooch | 2010

12 X 7.5 X 2 CM

Wool, synthetic fiber, nickel silver, stainless steel, printed
photo; felted, ironed, fabricated, riveted, screwed

PHOTOS BY ARTIST

Justyna Truchanowska

Neckpiece No. 4 | 2009

60 X 25 X 5 CM

Merino fleece, thread, sterling silver; wet felted

MAIN PHOTO BY ARTIST
DETAIL PHOTO BY GERRY MORGAN

Lee Schein

Untitled | 2005

80 X 18 X 3 CM

Merino fleece, Shetland fleece, yarn threads, clay, leather; wet felted, needle felted, hand felted, embroidered, hand fabricated

PHOTOS BY ARTIST

Gil Leitersdorf
Architectural E-Cut Version of a Tulip | 2009
80 X 90 X 90 CM

Merino wool, alpaca tops, Bluefaced Leicester fleece, camel hair, massam tops, white tussah silk; handmade, wet felted, folded, cut

PHOTOS BY RAN ERDA

Jenne Giles
Hibiscus Rose | 2006
152.4 X 20.3 X 0.6 CM
Merino wool, tussah silk, silk chiffon; nuno techniques
PHOTO BY ARTIST

Janet Crowe
Untitled | 2007
33 X 28 X 8 CM
Merino fleece; wet felted
PHOTO BY ARTIST

Ulrike V. Kutzleben-Hausen

Etwas Zurückhaltend | 2009

25 X 140 CM

Merino wool, natural dyed silk; nuno techniques, shibori

PHOTOS BY ARTIST

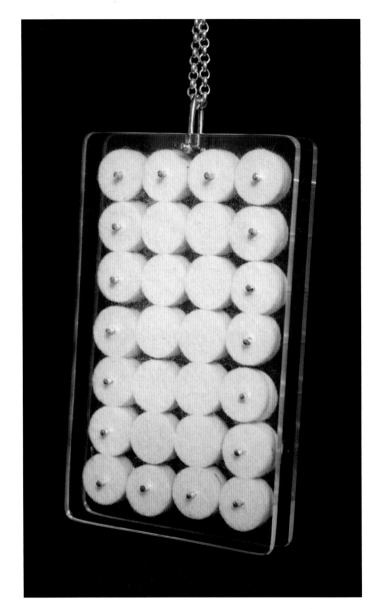

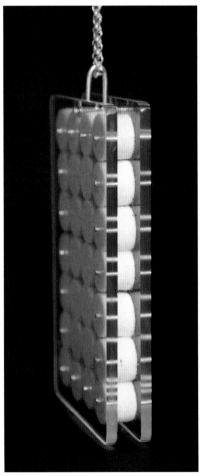

Leigh Wagner

Round & Round Pendant | 2010

9.3 X 5 X 1.2 CM

Industrial felt, acrylic, sterling silver; polished, riveted

Pia Wallén

Slitz Bracelet | 1997

BAND: 1.5 CM WIDE

100% wool, sterling silver; handmade

PHOTO BY FREDRIK LIEBERATH/LINK

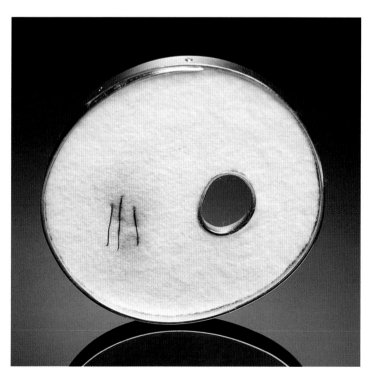

Kristin Mitsu Shiga

Stitch Brooch | 2007

6 X 7 X 0.8 CM

Sterling silver, wool felt, steel; fabricated

PHOTO BY DAN KVITKA

Miriam Verbeek
Chain | 2002
45 X 15 CM
Merino wool; wet felted
PHOTO BY ARTIST

Christina A. Hogan

Roman Chain with Monkey's Fist Closures | 2009

62.5 X 33 X 10 CM

Peruvian highland wool yarn, sterling silver, fine silver, patina;
knitted, fulled, woven, dapped, plied, knotted, soldered

PHOTO BY DAVID NEVALA

Margit Seland

Spor III | 2005

JACKET: SIZE MEDIUM; BAG: 35 X 40 X 10 CM

Wool, wool felt; knitted, felted, stitched, layered

PHOTO BY ARTIST

Weidesign

Handbag 1-005 | 2009

20 X 25 X 7 CM

Industrial wool felt; stitched

PHOTO BY AD BOGAARD

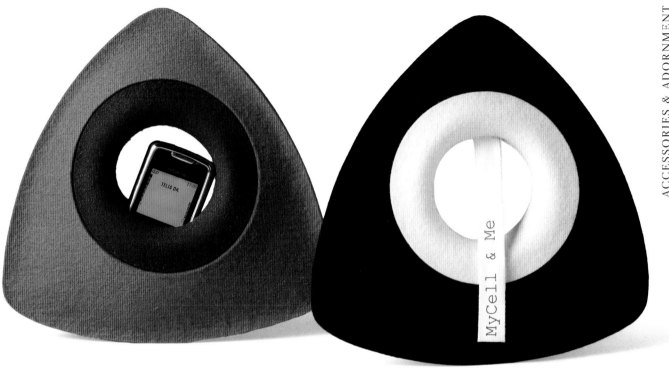

Inge Lindqvist
Karina Noyons
MyCell Wristbag | 2008
21 X 21 X 7 CM
Industrial felt; steamed, shaped
PHOTOS BY DORTHE KROGH

MyCell *is a cross between a bracelet and a bag. It's designed to hold small items such as lipstick, keys, and a cellphone, so that the wearer's hands are free.* —IL & KN

139

Charlotte Buch
Untitled | 2008

85 X 200 CM

Merino wool, silk chiffon; handmade, shibori, dyed, pleated

PHOTOS BY PERNILLE KAALUND

Emma Jackson
Charcoal Ripple Bag | 2007
30 X 30 CM
Merino wool, silk chiffon, silk fibers; hand dyed, wet
felted, nuno techniques, shibori
PHOTO BY ELLIE GIBBON

Yeseul Seo

The Reborn Rabbit | 2009

25 X 14 X 15 CM

Wool, sterling silver, cloth, doll eyes;
needle felted, sewn, fabricated

PHOTO BY KWANG CHOON PARK

Sarah Fox

Home Bracelet | 2008

10 X 6.3 X 9 CM

Wool, sterling silver; wet felted, dry felted,
hand fabricated, metal techniques

PHOTO BY DAN KVITKA

Noellynn Pepos

Untitled | 2009

DIMENSIONS VARY

Merino wool, silk, mohair; nuno techniques

PHOTO BY ARTIST

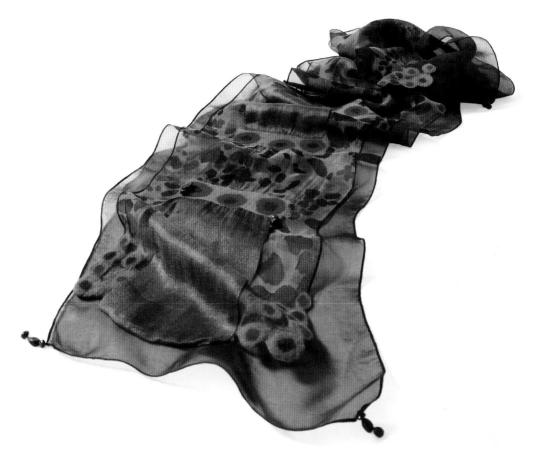

Maude Bath

From the Woven Weaves Series: Desert Stones | 2008

220 X 35 CM

Australian merino wool, silk organza,
silk chiffon, silk gauze, Australian native seeds;
woven, decorated, nuno techniques

FABRIC PRINTED AND HAND PAINTED BY LIZ WAUCHOPE
PHOTOS BY MALCOLM DOWNES

Agostina Zwilling
feltrigami Spacebag | 2008
55 X 50 X 22 CM
Merino fleece, linen thread, raku ceramic inserts, leather
handles, cotton lining; wet felted, stitched, embroidered
PHOTO BY MARCO BRAVI

I took advantage of the weightlessness of wool when making this piece. Although the material starts out shapeless, it can be transformed into a dense form with relatively crisp lines while maintaining its initial softness. —MG

Maricha Genovese
Under Pressure | 2009
30 X 25 X 4 CM
Wool, thread, sterling silver; needle felted, stitched, soldered, cast
PHOTO BY KEN YANOVIAK

Tara Turner
Untitled | 2008
20 X 4 X 3 CM
Merino wool, sterling silver;
wet felted, sawed, wire wrapped
PHOTO BY HAP SAKWA

Loretta Oliver
Shadow Tracks | 2009
188 X 25 X 0.3 CM
Merino wool fiber, silk fabric, cotton and wool yarns;
painted, partially hand woven, nuno techniques, shibori
PHOTO BY CLAUDE OLIVER

Irit Dulman
Untitled | 2008
30 X 43 X 14 CM
Bergschaf wool, New
Zealand wool; wet felted
PHOTOS BY ARI AVITS & IDAN LEVY

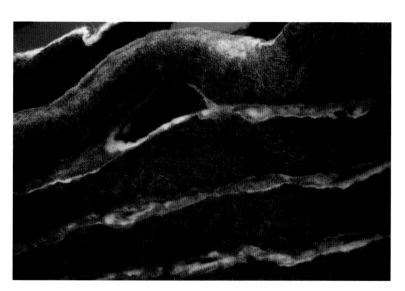

Janice Arnold

Necklett | 2006

17.8 X 45.7 CM

Merino fleece, rayon velvet,
silk fiber; hand felted

PHOTOS BY BOB IYALL

Liz Clay

Sculptured Scarf | 2007

110 X 12 CM

Merino fleece, cashmere, silk,
wool, silk georgette; embroidered,
wet felted, nuno techniques

PHOTO BY CLIVE BOURSNELL

Caius Kull
Tiina Kull
Untitled | 2009
NECKLACE: 21 CM IN DIAMETER; EACH EARRING: 3 CM IN DIAMETER
Merino wool, silver, pearls; wet felted
PHOTO BY DIANA KULL

José Vermeij

Global Warming Bracelet | 2010

3 X 10 X 10 CM

Merino fleece, brass wire mesh;
wet felted, fired, dapped

PHOTO BY ARTIST

Tara Turner

Untitled | 2008

20 X 4 X 4 CM

Merino wool, sterling silver; wet felted,
sawed, wire wrapped, soldered

PHOTO BY HAP SAKWA

Lisa Klakulak

Petalous | 2007

127 X 15.2 CM

Merino wool fleece, silk fabric, glass seed beads, labradorite stone beads; wet felted, naturally dyed, machine embroidered, hand stitched, beaded

PHOTOS BY TOM MILLS

Holland Webster
Untitled | 2008
20.3 X 22.9 X 8.9 CM
Industrial felt, copper, magnets,
liver of sulfur; hand fabricated
PHOTO BY ARTIST

Kachina Martin
Autumn Pebbles | 2009
20 X 162 CM
Wool roving, gauze; nuno techniques, hand dyed, manipulated
PHOTOS BY KEVIN BRETT

Susan Nichols

Red Bubble Scarf | 2009

90 CM LONG

Wool; knitted, shibori, wet felted

PHOTO BY TERENCE BOGUE

Laura Kochevar

Flamenco Scarf | 2010

142.2 X 17.8 CM

Merino fiber; wet felted, stretched

PHOTO BY ARTIST

Joanne Haywood

Black Sun | 2009

8.5 X 7 X 2 CM

Merino fleece, silver, cotton, alpaca yarn, natural dyes;
wet felted, formed, fused, oxidized, stitched, crocheted, dyed

PHOTO BY ARTIST

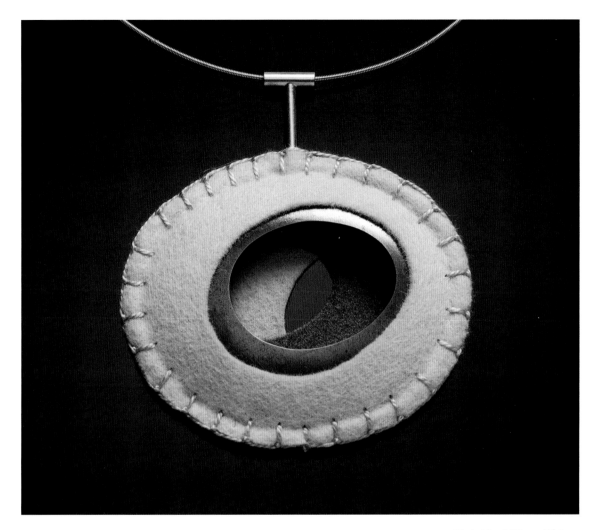

Kristin Mitsu Shiga
Green Cosie | 2008
9 X 9 X 1 CM
Copper, sterling silver, wool felt, acrylic, cotton thread;
fabricated, hydraulic pressed, flocked, stitched, oxidized
PHOTO BY DAN KVITKA

Rachel Timmins
Choke | 2008
30 X 51 X 1 CM
Merino wool, tamboo; wet felted, needle felted
PHOTOS BY ARTIST

Choke is about restriction in adornment. I use wool, a natural, comforting material, in a way that makes both the wearer and the viewer feel constricted. My goal is to raise questions about materialism and how our society views certain forms of adornment. —RT

Sara Owens
Hive (Brooch) | 2010
5.5 X 5.5 X 3.5 CM
Shetland wool, sink filter, brass wire; needle felted
PHOTO BY JOHN MCLELLAN

Catherine Drieux of ARCHIbidouilles
Ribambelle | 2009
225 X 45 CM
Felt; laser cut
PHOTOS BY BAS VAN ABEL

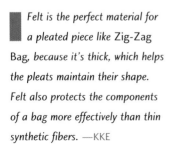
Felt is the perfect material for a pleated piece like Zig-Zag Bag, *because it's thick, which helps the pleats maintain their shape. Felt also protects the components of a bag more effectively than thin synthetic fibers.* —KKE

Kim Ki Eun
Zig-Zag Bag | 2005
55 X 39 X 11 CM
Industrial felt, steel, silk thread, sheepskin; hand-sewn, stitched
PHOTO BY ARTIST

Beth Burns
Untitled | 2010
38.1 X 177.8 CM
Merino wool, Tencel; hand woven, felted, dyed
PHOTOS BY J. AARON TROTMAN

Anne M. Fiala
Ophelia Necklace | 2008
DIMENSIONS VARY
Industrial felt; laser cut
PHOTOS BY ARTIST

Binary Neckpiece *resulted from my experiments with laser-cut felt. I love the idea of applying a technology that's known for its precision to a soft, natural material. The necklace's design spells out "What?" in binary code.* —ME

Maria Eife
Binary Neckpiece | 2009
24 X 0.3 CM
Industrial wool felt; laser cut
PHOTO BY ARTIST

Hut Up
Belly Bag AB 10/12 | 2010
DIMENSIONS VARY
Merino wool
DESIGNED BY CHRISTINE BIRKLE
PHOTO BY ARTIST

Leiko Uchiyama
Bag | 2008
40 X 30 X 12 CM
Merino wool; dyed, wet felted
PHOTO BY KAZUHIRO KOBUSHI

Felicitas Weitkämper
Nuno Scarf | 2009
25 X 130 CM
Merino wool, double-faced silk
gauze; nuno techniques
PHOTOS BY ARTIST

Cynthia Toops
Ribbed Bracelet | 2008
10 X 9.5 X 6 CM
Merino and other fleeces; dry needle felted
PHOTO BY DOUG YAPLE

Lynda Watson
Seabright Seaweed | 2008
15.5 X 15.5 X 1.5 CM
Wool fleece, sterling silver; needle felted, fabricated
PHOTO BY R.R. JONES

Rachel Timmins
Pods Give Birth, Too | 2008
198 X 15 X 15 CM
Merino wool, wool yarn; wet felted, dyed
PHOTO BY ARTIST

Eun Yeong Jeong
Wear it! Feel it! | 2007
14 X 5 X 3 CM
Wool, cactus, copper; needle felted
PHOTO BY ARTIST

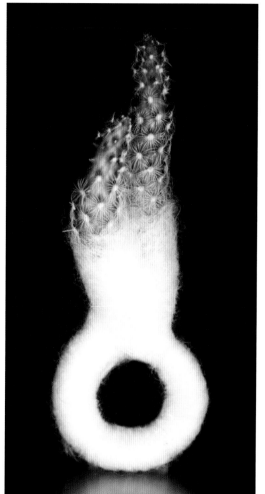

Hung-Ting Lee
Brooch | 2010
3 X 4.5 X 2.5 CM
Corriedale fleece, bead, bronze, thread,
sulfur patina; cast, spray-painted, felted
PHOTO BY WEN CHENG CHIEH

Eun Yeong Jeong

Those Sweet Words | 2008

55 X 23 X 5 CM

Love letters, wool, nylon thread, sterling silver;
needle felted, stitched, dyed, embroidered

PHOTOS BY ARTIST

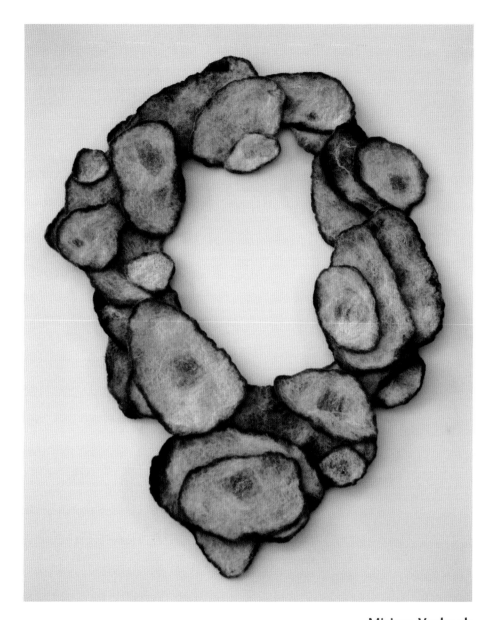

Miriam Verbeek
Ice Floe | 2008
53 X 35 X 1.2 CM
Silk, metal silk, merino wool; wet felted

Ulrike V. Kutzleben-Hausen

(T)Raumbild II | 2008

230 X 150 CM

Merino wool, natural dyed silk; nuno techniques, shibori

PHOTO BY ARTIST

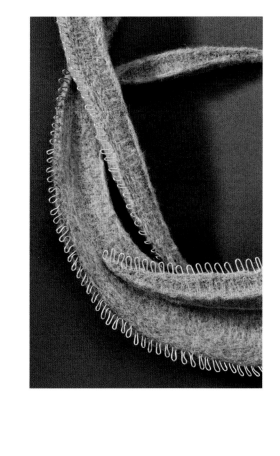

Lynda Watson

The Cactus in the Window | 2009

25 X 35 X 4 CM

Merino wool fleece, fine silver; needle felted, dyed, fabricated

PHOTOS BY R.R. JONES

Sylvie Lupien
Necklace | 2009
32 CM IN DIAMETER
Merino wool, sterling silver; hand felted, soldered, embroidered
PHOTO BY DAVID BISHOP

Sylvie Lupien

Mobile-Necklace | 2009

38 X 31 X 2.5 CM

Merino wool, sterling silver, brass, peridot, garnet,
citrine, iolite, glass beads, cotton embroidery wire;
hand felted, soldered, set, polished, embroidered

PHOTO BY DAVID BISHOP

Naomi Landig

Crook | 2008

7 X 6 X 3 CM

Merino wool, sterling silver, rubber band

PHOTO BY MARIA PHILLIPS

Dena J. Gershon

Montaña de Oro | 2007

196 X 28 X 11.5 CM

Merino wool, Romney wool, mohair, silk,
electrical wire; wet felted, hand dyed

PHOTO BY HILARY KENNEDY

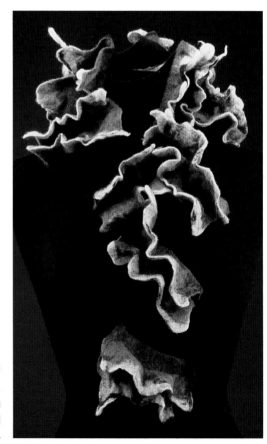

Hansard Welsh Design

Truffle Lei | 2002

122 X 17 X 7 CM

Merino wool; wet felted

PHOTO BY DEAN POWELL

Dagmar Binder
Coral Scarves | 2004
EACH: 220 X 35 CM
Merino wool; wet felted
PHOTO BY ARTIST

Holland Webster

Untitled | 2008

33 X 17.8 X 5.7 CM

Industrial felt, copper, liver of sulfur; hand fabricated

PHOTO BY ARTIST

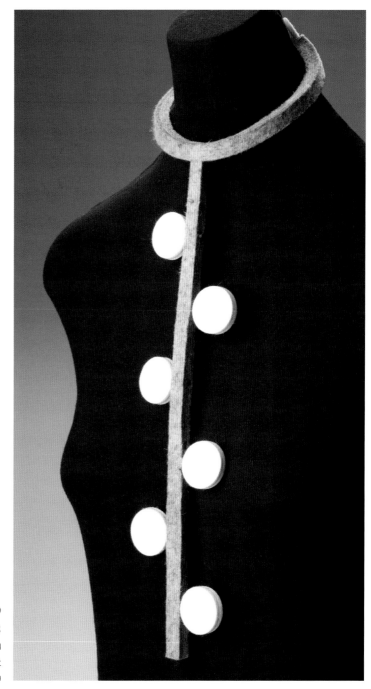

Rosalyn Y. Weintraub
Orte Necklace | 2008
33 X 8 X 1.3 CM
Recycled industrial felt, steel structure; die cut
PHOTO BY SHELL HEMSLEIGH

Alexandra Luengen
Untitled | 2009
243 X 46 CM
Merino tops, silk fibers, silk paper, silk chiffon;
hand dyed, wet felted, nuno techniques
PHOTO BY INES HEIDER

Christine Sinclair

Raku Windows | 2009

178 X 18 CM

Silk gauze, merino wool; nuno techniques, shibori

PHOTO BY BARBARA TALBOTT

Emma Jackson

Hot Orange Cobweb Wrap and Bag | 2007

WRAP: 180 CM LONG; BAG: 30 X 18 CM

Merino wool and silk blend, cobweb felt,
velvet; hand wet felted, machine embroidered

PHOTO BY ELLIE GIBBON

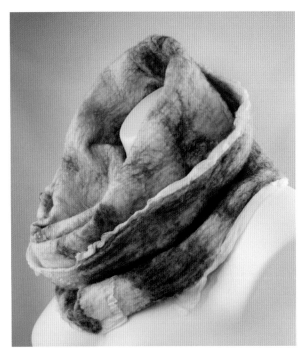

Krista Gorrell

Infinity Circle Scarf in Natural | 2010

45 X 37 X 37 CM

Merino fleece, Bluefaced Leicester fleece, silk; wet felted, nuno techniques

PHOTO BY ARTIST

Tammy L. Deck

Fossil Cuff | 2008

17.8 CM IN DIAMETER

Merino cross fleece, vintage button, crinoid fossils, vintage beads, rhinestones, faux pearls, labradorite beads, nylon thread; wet felted, stitched

PHOTO BY ARTIST

Zhavoronkova Tatiana

Orenburg | 2009

160 X 30 CM

Wensleydale fleece; wet felted, cobweb techniques

PHOTO BY BOYARINOV DMITRY

gewoon

Robin Necklace | 2009

35 CM IN DIAMETER

Wool; die cut, stitched

PHOTO BY MONIQUE TEUNISSEN

Michela Gregoretti (Tinakela)
Circle in Circle | 2008
45 X 45 CM
Merino wool, Bergschaf wool; wet felted
PHOTOS BY URBAN GOLOB

Maja Gecic
Necklace | 2010
160 CM LONG
Serbian wool; wet felted, stitched
PHOTO BY NENAD ZLATANOCIC

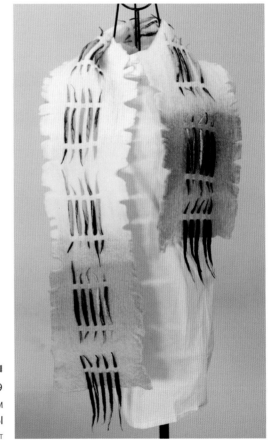

Chin-Mei Wu
The Scarf of Railway Beggarticks | 2009
135 X 22 CM
Wool
PHOTO BY ARTIST

Jenne Giles
Tendril Scarf: Oat | 2009
177.8 X 76.2 X 0.6 CM
Merino wool, bombyx silk; wet felted, shibori
PHOTO BY ARTIST

Margit Seland
Plus | 2008
LARGEST: 55 X 35 X 35 CM
Wool felt, industrial felt; layered, screen-printed, stitched
PHOTO BY ARTIST

Jens A. Clausen
Moon | 2008
5.1 X 5.1 X 0.9 CM
Lamb's wool, sterling silver box, stainless
steel wire; dyed, needle felted
PHOTOS BY ARTIST

Fanny Sophie Gjestland
Object for Daydreaming | 2001
15 X 15 X 80 CM
Wool, string, silicone ear plugs; wet felted, threaded
PHOTO BY HASSE NIELSEN

Vilte Kazlauskaite
Iris Wattii | 2010
110 X 25 CM
Merino wool, silk chiffon; wet felted, dyed with plants
PHOTO BY ARTIST

Jennifer Moss
Respiration | 2008
40 X 30 X 5 CM
Merino wool, sterling silver; wet felted, needle felted, forged
PHOTO BY ARTIST

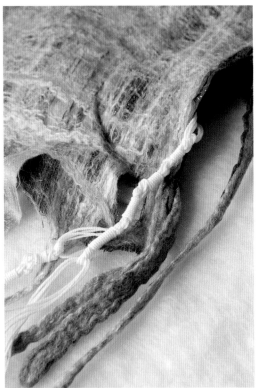

Patricia Frank Sher

Waters of Babylon Tallit | 2009

55.9 X 203.2 CM

Alpaca and silk tussah roving blend, silk chiffon, torn silk,
silk and metallic embroidery floss, amethyst beads, kosher
tzitzit; nuno techniques, stitched, embroidered, hand knotted

PHOTOS BY BRIAN ALPERT

Sheila Ahern
Midnight Wrap | 2010
DIMENSIONS NOT AVAILABLE
Merino fleece, silk tops, silk
chiffon; nuno techniques
PHOTO BY JOANNA TOMASZEWSKA

Julia Romanova
Lagoon | 2009
40 X 140 CM
Merino fleece; wet
felted, embroidered
PHOTO BY ARTIST

Chien-Ching Liao

Maturity II | 2010

10 X 11 X 1.5 CM

Felt, silver

PHOTO BY ARTIST

Michele A. Friedman

Olive Branch Brooch | 2006

9 X 3.5 CM

Wool felt, sterling silver, 18-karat gold bi-metal, gold-plated brass
screws; hand manipulated, set, cast, fabricated, cold connected

PHOTO BY HAP SAKWA

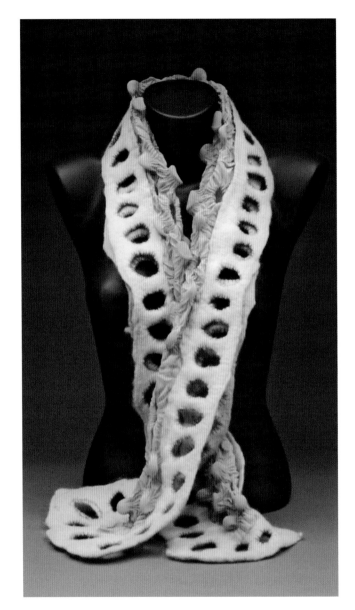

Lily Liu

S 302 | 2005

198.1 X 25.4 CM

Merino fleece, polyester, rayon thread; dyed,
nuno technique, heat set, wet felted, stitched

PHOTO BY JOHN HASEGAWA

Chiu-Tzu-Ying

Complex | 2009

35 X 40 X 8 CM

Merino fleece; wet felted

PHOTOS BY ARTIST

Lisa Klakulak
Untitled | 2010

EACH: 7.6 X 7.6 X 0.6 CM

Finn/Rambouillet wool fleece, silk fabric, reclaimed eyes of hook-and-eye sets, carnelian stone beads, glass seed beads, sterling silver hoops; naturally dyed, wet felted, free-motion machine embroidered, hand stitched and beaded

PHOTO BY STEVE MANN

Charlotte Buch
Untitled | 2008
45 X 200 CM
Merino wool, silk chiffon; handmade,
shibori, dyed, pleated
PHOTO BY PERNILLE KAALUND

Brigit Daamen
Woldolomiet | 2008
EACH: 3 X 3 X 2 CM
Wool felt, silicon, alpaca; glued
PHOTO BY ARTIST

Weidesign
Basket 3-002 | 2009
35 X 43 CM
Industrial wool felt, natural hemp; stitched
PHOTOS BY AD BOGAARD

Jean Gauger

Nuno Felted Buckeye Butterfly Shawl | 2008

61 X 208 CM

Merino wool, silk gauze, habotai silk, silk handkerchiefs,
tussah silk roving; hand dyed, nuno techniques

PHOTOS BY ARTIST

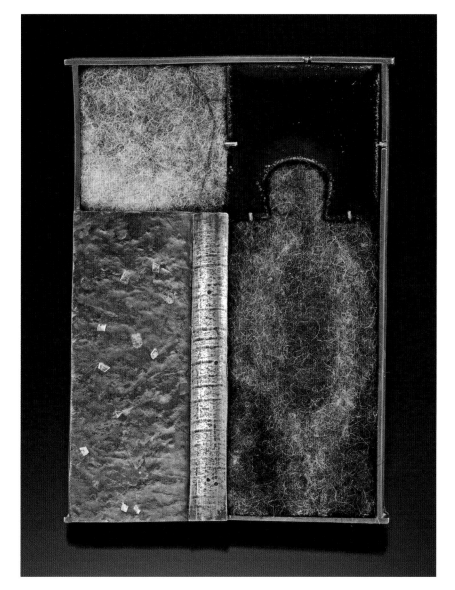

Thea Clark

Solitary One (Homage to R. Tamayo) | 2008

7.6 X 5 X 0.9 CM

Merino and Romney roving, silver, enamel on copper, 24-karat gold; wet
felted, needle felted, inlay felted, formed, enameled, textured, soldered

PHOTO BY LARRY SANDERS

Nurjamal Asangulova
Gauze | 2010
130 X 35 X 0.4 CM
Merino fleece, cotton; dyed, wet felted
PHOTO BY ERKIN BOLJUROV

Gill Brooks
Octopus Tentacles | 2009
10 X 150 CM
Merino wool; shibori dyed
PHOTO BY JIM SMITH

Katie Mawson

Tyre Scarf | 2009

166 CM LONG

Merino lamb's wool; knitted, felted

PHOTO BY ANDRA NELKI

Irit Dulman
Untitled | 2008
29 X 40 X 14 CM
Bergschaf wool, New Zealand wool; wet felted
PHOTOS BY ARI AVITS & IDAN LEVY

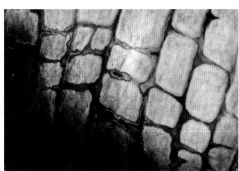

Lynda Watson

Eucalyptus Neckpiece | 2008

21 X 42 X 2 CM

Silk, merino wool fleece, sterling silver; needle felted, fabricated

PHOTO BY R.R. JONES

Heather Hall

Trumpet Vine Garland | 2009

5 X 5 X 183 CM

Merino fleece, cotton thread; wet felted, stitched

PHOTO BY ARTIST

Lilyana Bekic
Matris | 2007
20.3 X 53.3 X 8.9 CM
Fur felt, silk cocoons; hand dyed,
blocked, hand formed, hand stitched
PHOTO BY ARTIST

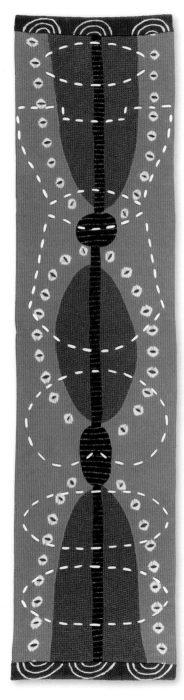

Kathryn Walter
FELT Quilt #1 | 2009
160 X 134.6 CM
Industrial wool felt remnants,
cotton backing; machine stitched
PHOTO BY DIANA BRAUN-WOODBURY

Jean Williams Cacicedo
Chart | 2007
127 X 45.7 CM
Wool; felted, dyed, slashed, stitched, pieced
PHOTO BY ARTIST

Uta Marschmann

Wall Carpet: Word Performance | 2008

160 X 40 CM

Merino fleece, natural indigo; wet felted, dyed,
reserve technique

PHOTOS BY ALEXANDER HEUBERGER

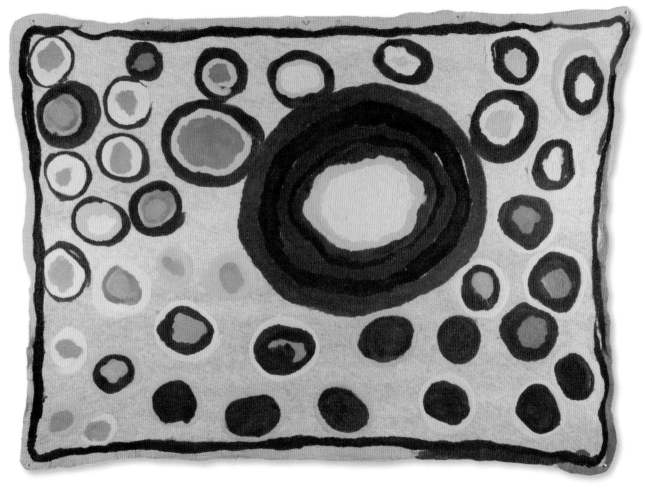

Walya Mitchell

Kunyma Tjukurrpa | 2009

155 X 214 CM

Merino wool; felted, dyed

PHOTO BY GARY PROCTOR
COURTESY OF THE WARBURTON ARTS PROJECT, WARBURTON RANGES, AUSTRALIA

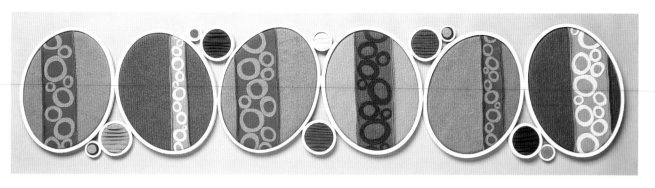

Chandra Stubbs

Between the Lines #2: Decorative Wall Hanging | 2009

35.5 X 162.5 CM

Merino fleece, porcelain clay; dyed, needle felted, thrown, altered, and
extruded porcelain, clear celadon glaze; gas fired, cone 9

PHOTO BY RICHARD HELLYER

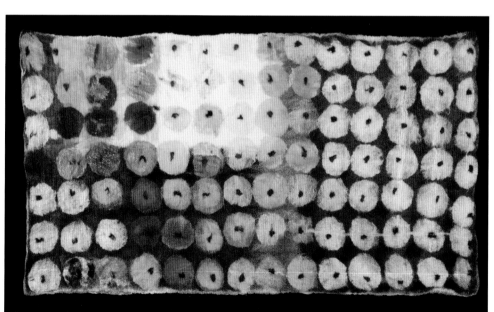

Claudia Hoffberg

Glow | 2009

28 X 50 CM

Merino, silk, Tencel;
hand dyed, wet felted

PHOTO BY SCOTT MCCUE

Michelle Jarvis
Red Dot Panel | 2004
100 X 120 CM
Industrial felt; printed, embroidered
PHOTO BY ARTIST

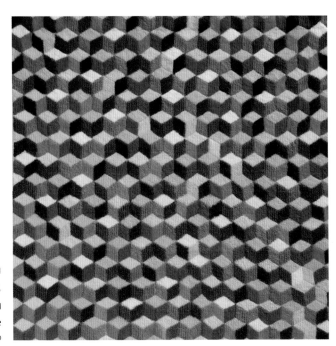

Ursula Jaton
Felted Quilt | 2006
159 X 163 CM
Merino fleece, soap; pre-felt technique
PHOTO BY ANTONIO MOLLO

Philip O'Reilly
Color and Interstices | 2000
350 X 350 X 3.5 CM
Recycled wool felt; needle felted, embroidered
PHOTOS BY ARTIST

Karina Eskilsson

Lingonberry Tufts | 2003

60 X 90 X 0.5 CM

Natural wool; hand felted, hand dyed

Aija Baumane
The Changing World Is Eternal | 2007
185 X 118 CM
Merino fleece; dry felted, stitched

Ulrike V. Kutzleben-Hausen
Kimono | 2007
140 X 160 CM
Merino wool, natural dyed silk;
nuno techniques, shibori
PHOTOS BY ARTIST

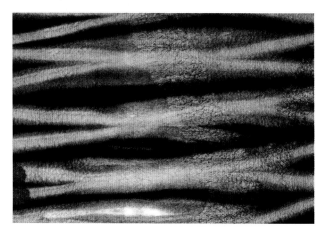

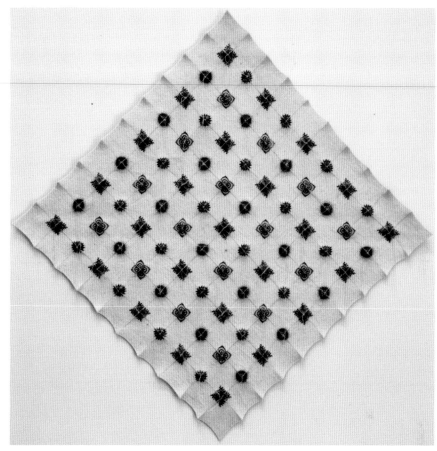

Chung-Im Kim
meiosis | 2007
69 X 69 X 3 CM
Industrial felt, embroidery
thread; printed, cut, stitched
PHOTOS BY ARTIST

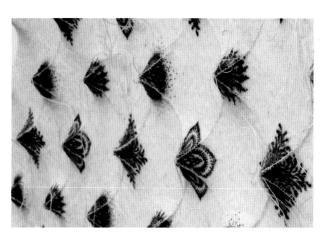

H. Nurgül Begiç

Ceremony Caftan of Ottoman Padisashes | 2010

115 X 96 X 0.3 CM

Merino fleece, handmade felt; wet felted, dyed, appliqué

PHOTO BY ERENCAN BEGIÇ

Roza Makashova
Shyrdak | 2009
110 X 240 CM
Wool fleece; wet felted, stitched
PHOTO BY EVGENIY SYCHEV

Hope Gelfand Alcorn

Rhythms | 2001

121.9 X 91.4 CM

Industrial wool, acrylic paint;
negative transfer with stencils

PHOTO BY ARTIST

Felt plays an important role in my wall coverings and toys. It's a soft, flexible material that gives tenderness and warmth to each piece, which is important because these items are created for children. —OR

Olesya Roskos

Wall Covering with Toys: Fairy World #1 | 2008

100 X 109 CM

Wool fleece; wet felted

PHOTO BY EVGENIY SYCHEV

Robin Wiltse
Fish Felt Series #5 | 2010
137.2 X 73.7 CM
Merino and Corriedale fleece; needle
felted, wet felted, stretched
PHOTOS BY ARTIST

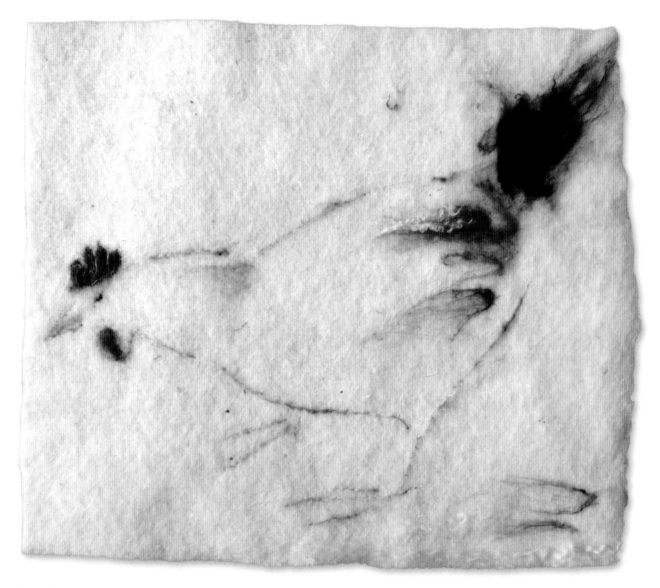

Ali Brown

Chick, Chick, Chicken | 2010

108 X 86 CM

Welsh fleece, industrial felt, silk fibers,
Finn fleece, local fleece; needle felted

PHOTO BY ARTIST

Heather Belcher

Holding the Coffee | 2008

80 X 115 CM

Merino fleece; wet felted

PHOTO BY DAVID RAMKALAWON

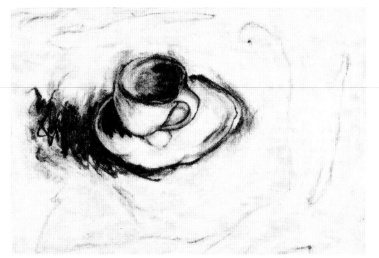

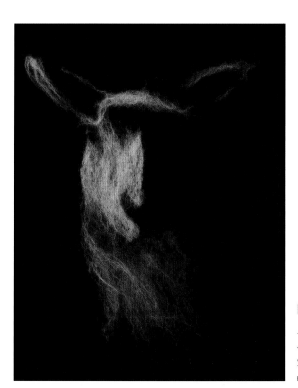

Rebecca Utecht

Portrait of Lena | 2009

43 X 33 CM

Shetland fleece; wet felted

PHOTO BY PETRONELLA YTSMA

Chung-Im Kim

in the midst | 2009

202 X 157 X 12 CM

Industrial felt, embroidery
thread; printed, cut, stitched

PHOTO BY ARTIST

With in the midst, I'm expressing my close connection to my material. Felt is endlessly fascinating to me because of its physicality and shape-forming ability. —CIM

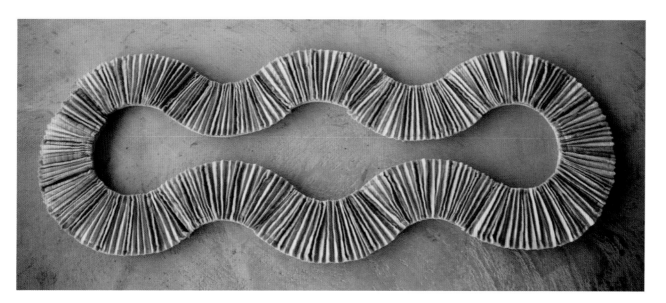

Kerstin Lindström
Lucky Loop | 2007
80 X 240 CM
Felt, wooden plate; dyed, plissé
PHOTO BY ARTIST

Jean Williams Cacicedo
The Swimmer/The Three Sisters | 2009
20 X 20 CM
Wool; woven, felted, dry needle felted, stitched
PHOTO BY ARTIST

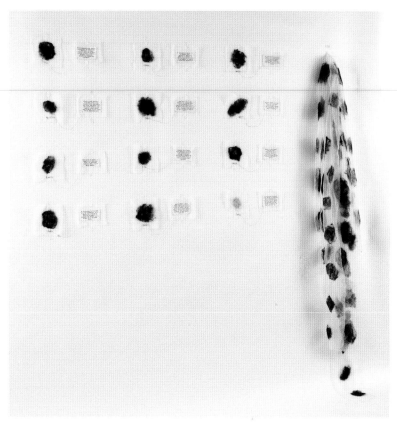

Tiziana Abretti

Contemporary Shroud | 2009

150 X 150 X 10 CM

Organza, handmade paper, raw wool, silk plaster,
thread; embroidered, nuno techniques, printed

PHOTOS BY ARTIST

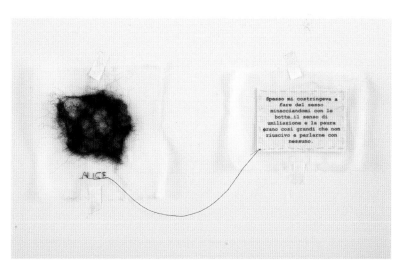

Elizabeth Holland

Kungkarrangkalpa Kurrualla | 2010

170 X 180 CM

Merino wool; felted, dyed

PHOTO BY GARY PROCTOR
COURTESY OF THE WARBURTON ARTS PROJECT, WARBURTON RANGES, AUSTRALIA

Joseph Young
Untitled | 2008
120 X 120 CM
Norwegian C-1/Pelsull fleece; wet felted, stitched

Sharron Parker
Written in Stone IV | 2009
97 X 124 X 5 CM
Wool, yarn; wet felted, stitched
PHOTO BY JAMES LINCON

Barbara Matera
Onda Negata—Wave Denied | 2009
30 X 400 X 4 CM
Carded wool, cotton thread;
wet felted, stitched, tied
PHOTO BY ARTIST

Brigitta Varadi
Lough Ree | 2008

630 X 165 X 1.5 CM

Merino and Corriedale wool, silk, metal thread,
iron; wet felted, dyed, stitched, hand forged

HAND FORGING BY JONATHAN BALL
PROJECT ASSISTANCE: PETER FULOP
PHOTOS BY EUNAN SWEENEY

Marian Jansen
Untitled | 2007
118 X 70 CM
Merino wool, silk, glass, stainless steel; wet felted
PHOTO BY ARTIST

Laura Pavilonyte
Migle Lebednykaite
Egle Ganda Bogdaniene
Felted Gardens I | 2006
120 X 160 X 5 CM
Merino wool; wet and dry felted
PHOTOS BY VAIVA ABROMAITYTE

We hand and needle felted white
wool to create this bas-relief,
which echoes the sculptures of the
Baroque masters. It's as if a historical
marble piece had been reincarnated in
felted wool. —LP, ML, EGB

Roderick Welch
You Are | 2005
106 X 48 CM
Finnish Landrace wool; wet felted
PHOTOS BY ARTIST

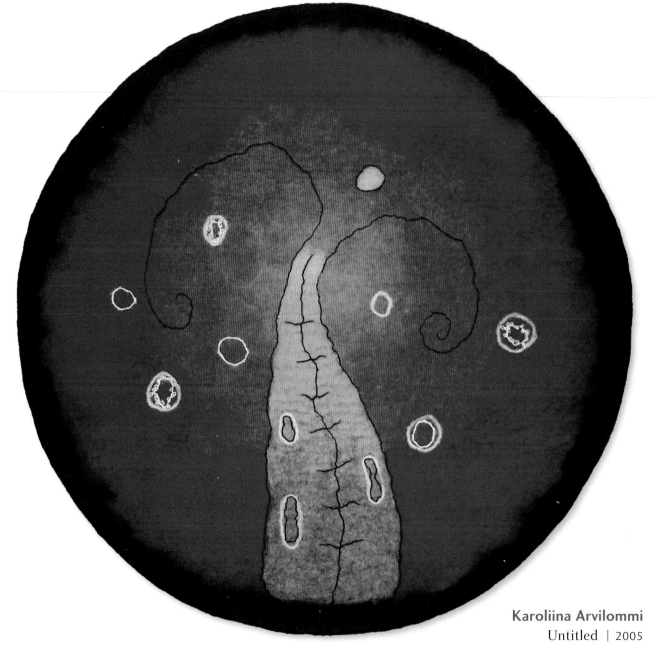

Karoliina Arvilommi
Untitled | 2005
80 CM IN DIAMETER
Finnish Landrace wool, yarn; wet felted
PHOTO BY RODERICK WELCH

Pamela H.W. Sager
One of These Things . . . | *2009*
213 X 61 X 5 CM
Industrial felt; dyed, cut
PHOTO BY ARTIST

> The word "folderol" means a showy, useless item. When I began making this piece, some people said that creating hundreds (actually thousands) of little felt balls seemed silly. I thought, they're right—this is a folderol. So the piece named itself. —MB

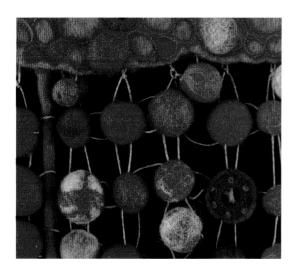

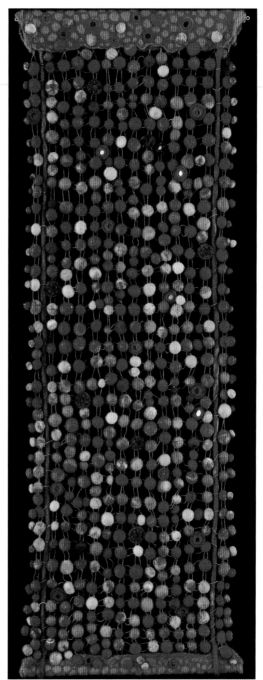

Marianne Burr
Folderol | 2005

132 X 46 X 2.5 CM

Wool roving, waxed linen thread, shisha mirrors; needle felted, wet felted, strung, machine stitched, hand stitched

PHOTOS BY FRANK ROSS

Hope Gelfand Alcorn
Migration Down Waterfall Number One | 2006
120.7 X 90.2 CM
Industrial wool, acrylic paint; negative transfer with stencils
PHOTOS BY SCOTT SMATHERS

Renee Harris
Three Hitching into the Night | 2008
40.6 X 40.6 X 0.6 CM
Merino fleece, cotton thread; wet felted, embroidered, stitched
PHOTO BY JAY BACHEMIN

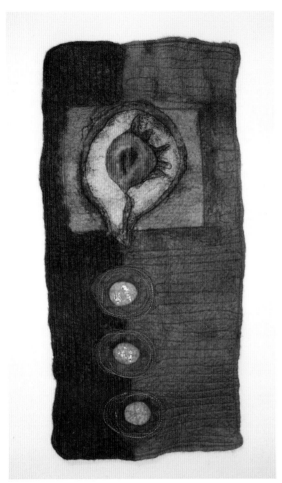

Cindy Obuck

Before It Blooms | 2009

30.5 X 66 CM

Merino wool, cotton thread, gold leaf;
wet felted, machine stitched, hand beaded

PHOTO BY ARTIST

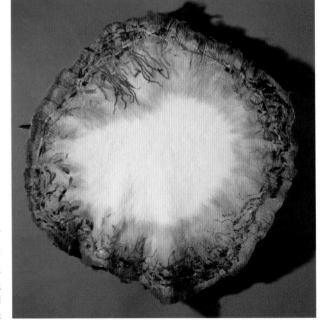

Teresa Glover

Reeds of Reflection | 2010

115 CM IN DIAMETER

Merino wool, alpaca, silk and wool fabrics, silk
thread, wool yarn; wet felted, hand dyed

PHOTO BY KRISTAL GILMOUR

Although of carpet quality and weight, these pieces are usually exhibited on the wall in a gallery space. Most people don't feel comfortable walking on art objects. —JJ

Jorie Johnson
View from Train Window Carpet Series: Orange Dusk | 2008
163 X 106 CM
Karakul, crossbreed fleece; hand felted
PHOTO BY YUZO TOYODA

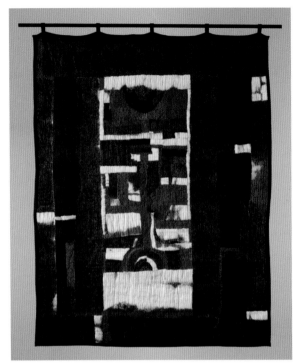

Lisa Kaser

Where to Begin | 2007

121.9 X 96.5 X 1.3 CM

Shetland wool, linen and cotton
thread; wet felted, stitched

PHOTO BY GRACE WESTON

*In dawn, each module represents an
independent soul—an individual entity with
its own unique power and energy. Together, these
individuals form a whole, like cells in a body.* —CIK

Chung-Im Kim

dawn | 2009

114 X 122 X 8 CM

Industrial felt, embroidery
thread; printed, cut, stitched

PHOTO BY ARTIST

Nola Hunt
Kungkarrangka | 2009
170 X 182 CM
Merino wool; felted, dyed

PHOTO BY GARY PROCTOR
COURTESY OF THE WARBURTON ARTS PROJECT, WARBURTON RANGES, AUSTRALIA

Morna Crites-Moore

Pieces of Dreams | 2003

43 X 50 CM

Recycled wool sweaters, repurposed silk, vintage velveteen, cotton, silk thread, antique buttons; felted, pressed, cut, stitched, quilted

PHOTO BY ARTIST

The idea for this piece came from the hundreds of recycled sweaters I've processed over the years. Stitching by hand, I combined scraps of wool from those sweaters, adding carefully chosen antique buttons. I built Pieces of Dreams *slowly, over a period of two years.* —MCM

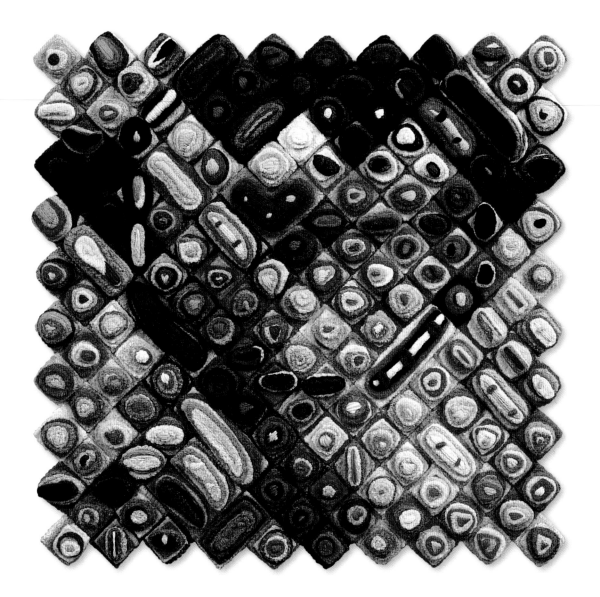

Susan Spencer Reckford

Chuck Up Close | 2005

35.5 X 37 X 2.5 CM

Merino wool, cotton muslin; machine
knitted, wet felted, stitched, embroidered

PHOTO BY PETE MOORE

Nola Hunt

Kapingka | 2009

186 X 178 CM

Merino wool; felted, dyed

PHOTO BY GARY PROCTOR
COURTESY OF THE WARBURTON ARTS PROJECT, WARBURTON RANGES, AUSTRALIA

Deb Donnelly
Setsuko | 2010
7.2 X 5.3 X 2.5 CM
Merino wool, gunma woven silk;
wet felted, hand dyed, shibori
PHOTO BY ARTIST

Karoliina Arvilommi

Growth | 2006

135 X 280 X 2 CM

Finnish Landrace wool, yarn; wet felted

PHOTO BY RODERICK WELCH

Sharron Parker
Copper Traces | 2009
71 X 147 X 5 CM
Wool, silk, yarn; wet felted, stitched, mounted
PHOTO BY LYNN RUCK

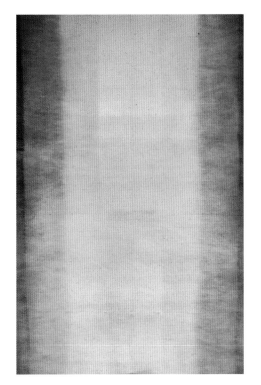

Inge Lindqvist
Fluid Yellow | 1997
180 X 140 CM
Industrial felt; dyed
PHOTO BY JAKOB H. HANSEN

Heather Belcher
Doll's Coat | 2008
50 X 60 CM
Merino fleece; wet felted
PHOTOS BY DAVID RAMKALAWON

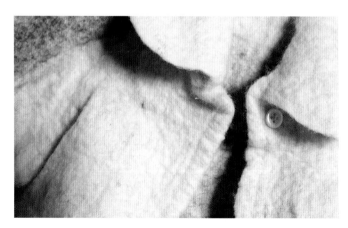

Kathleen Hill

Giant | 2000

162 X 73 X 3.5 CM

Romney wool, wool yarn, silk yarn, silk fibers; dyed, inlaid, wet felted, stitched, embroidered, re-felted

PHOTO BY LARRY DOELL

Ana Lisa Hedstrom

Ghost Forest | 2009

213 X 89 X 1.5 CM

Synthetic felt; hand stitched, dye sublimation transfer printed

PHOTO BY DON TUTTLE

Dagmar Binder
Untitled | 2009
118 X 63 X 7 CM
Merino wool; wet felted
PHOTO BY ARTIST

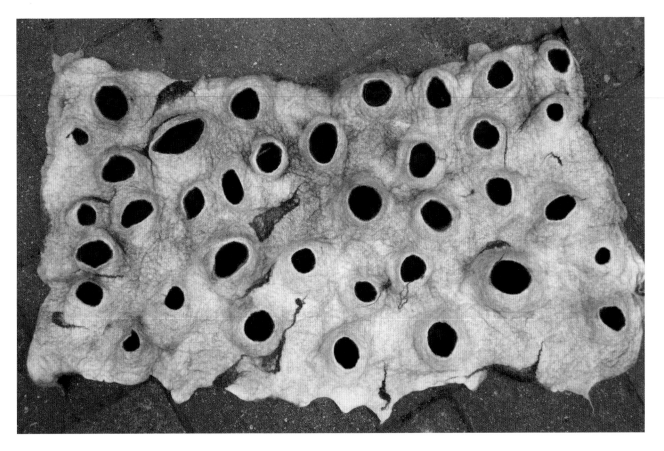

Elis Vermeulen
Barnacles | 2009
1.2 X 90 CM
Norwegian, Finn, Gotland, and La Plata wools; wet felted
PHOTOS BY ARTIST

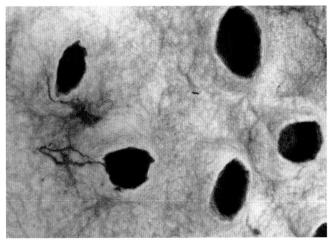

Sue Wheatley
Reductive Permutations | 2003
OVERALL: 5.7 X 5.5 X 0.6 M
Industrial felt, steel
PHOTO BY ARTIST

Angelika Werth
*From the Madeleines Series: Boxing
Dress for Marilyn Monroe* | 2010
SIZE 8
Wool, silk, silk velvet, suspenders, boxing gloves;
hand dyed, hand felted, constructed, stitched
PHOTO BY JEREMY ADDINGTON

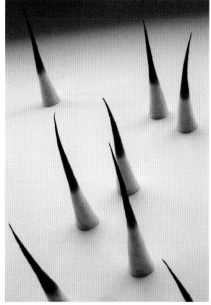

Anna Kristina Goransson
Untitled | 2007
150 X 215 X 25 CM
Merino fleece; wet felted, dyed
PHOTOS BY ARTIST

Dorie Van Dÿk
Seaweed | 2010
200 X 20 CM
Merino fleece, silk chiffon; hand dyed, wet felted, nuno techniques
PHOTOS BY ARTIST

Imogen Noble
Felt in the Landscape | 2006
25 M LONG
Blended merino fleece; wet felted
PHOTOS BY DOUGLAS NOBLE

Lyda Rump
Seaweed Brains | 2009
10 X 12 CM
Merino wool, silk; painted, dyed, wet felted
PHOTO BY TRUUS VISSER

Mel Miller
Object Reminiscent of Things Past, No. 5 | 2009
12.5 X 17 X 13 CM
Merino fleece, enamel, copper, sterling
silver; wet felted, stitched, repoussé
PHOTO BY JEREMY DILLON

Seeds *started as raw wool, which I punched thousands of times with a barbed needle. Working as a painter would, I applied, removed, and reapplied layers of color. I was intrigued by the contraction of the wool as it changed from soft wisps to compact concentrations of color and shape.* —JC

Jodi Colella
Seeds | 2008
VARIOUS SIZES
Wool roving; hand dyed, needle felted
PHOTO BY ARTIST

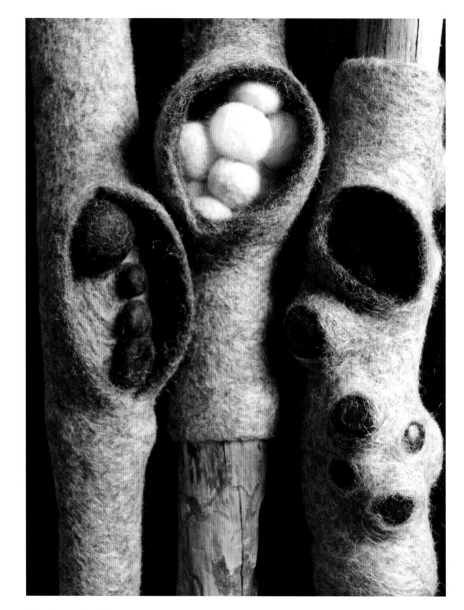

Andrea Graham
Liberatio Captivus | 2008
40 X 15 X 5 CM
Finnish Landrace wool, driftwood; marble resists, wet felted
PHOTO BY ARTIST

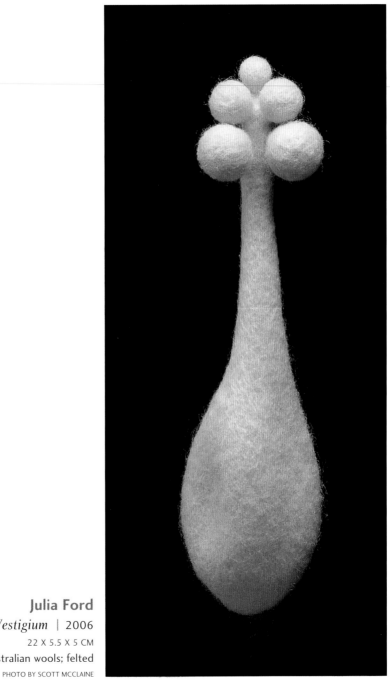

Julia Ford
Vestiges Series: Sprout, Vestigium | 2006
22 X 5.5 X 5 CM
Coopworth and Australian wools; felted
PHOTO BY SCOTT MCCLAINE

Bita Ghezelayagh
Felt Memories IX | 2009
102 X 116 CM
Felt, brass crowns, keys, tulips, wire mesh
PHOTO BY ARTIST

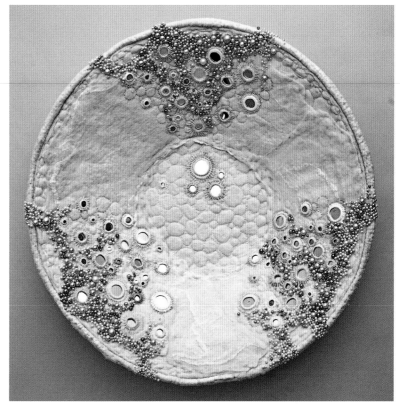

Marianne Burr

Celebration Bowl | 2008

51 CM IN DIAMETER

Merino wool, silk roving, shisha mirrors,
faux pearls; wet felted, machine stitched,
hand fabricated, hand stitched

PHOTOS BY FRANK ROSS

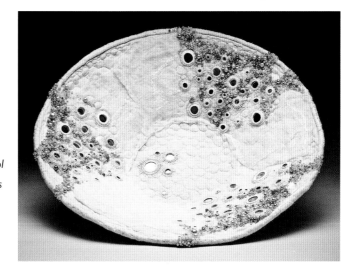

Celebration Bowl *is the joyous result of a
self-imposed challenge to create a three-
dimensional object from hand-felted merino wool
enhanced with silk roving. I sewed on the mirrors
and faux pearls individually, by hand.* —MB

Deborah C. Pope

Quixotic | 2008

68.6 X 20.3 X 20.3 CM

Merino wool, wire, cotton, silk, wool cloth, leather, paper clay, wood, straw, paper; wet felted, stitched, beaded, sculpted, painted

PHOTO BY LLOYD WILSON

Kate Church

Sgt. Pepper's Lonely Hearts Club | 2009

23 X 20 X 13 CM

Felted sweaters, various fabrics, silk flower petals, polymer clay, paper cone, gold leaf, wooden wheels, jeweler's chain, glass beads; dyed, stitched, painted, jointed

PHOTO BY ARTIST

Lisa Kaser
Carrying Stones from Along the Way | 2006
25.4 X 76.2 X 20.3 CM
Wool felt, wood, bone, linen, steel bristles, feathers, found objects, beeswax; wet felted, dyed, stitched, carved, pegged
PHOTOS BY BILL BAUCHHUBER

Jennifer Moss

Propagation | 2009

89 X 183 X 14 CM

Merino and Corriedale wool, wax, oil color; wet felted, needle felted, coated

PHOTOS BY ARTIST

Anna Kristina Goransson
Lightdrops | 2008

340 X 450 X 450 CM

Merino fleece; wet felted, dyed

PHOTOS BY ARTIST

Lightdrops *was inspired by memories of walking in the forest in the early morning. I was trying to capture the tranquility of those moments. Felt was the perfect material to use because of its lightness and softness.* —AKG

Jorie Johnson
Clifton Monteith

Winged Vessel II | 2004

19.1 X 13.3 X 13.5 CM

Wool felt, bast fibers, leaf, urushi lacquer

PHOTO BY JOHN R. WILLIAMS
COLLECTION OF THE COOPER-HEWITT, NATIONAL DESIGN MUSEUM

Gill Ferguson

Pebble Pots | 2008

EACH: 17 X 15 X 11 CM

Norwegian fleece, silk, Wensleydale curls; wet felted

PHOTO BY ROGER LEE

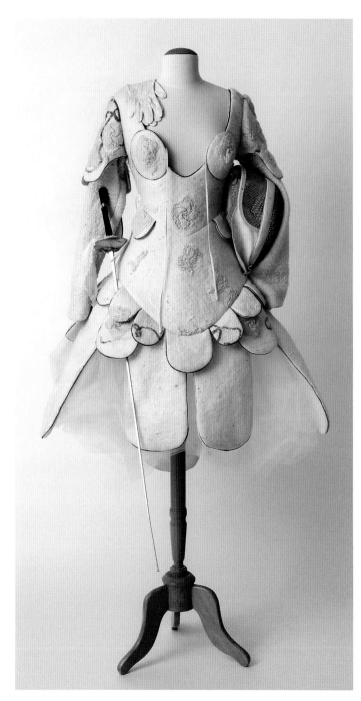

Angelika Werth

From the Madeleines Series: Fencing Dress for Joan of Arc | 2010

SIZE 6

Wool, silk, lace, metallic silk, tulle, épée, fencing mask; hand felted, constructed, stitched

PHOTO BY JEREMY ADDINGTON

Michelle Sales
Gravity K | 2009
12.7 X 7.6 X 10.2 CM
Romney fleece, rock, shells; dyed, stitched, pyrography
PHOTO BY JONATHAN SALES

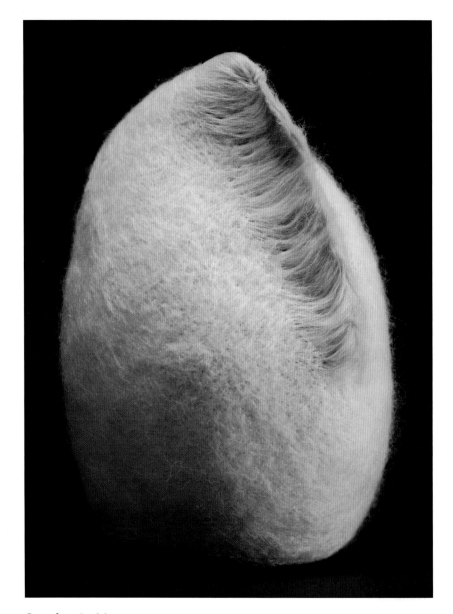

Stephanie Metz
Amorphozoa #3 | 2009
20 X 13.3 X 15.3 CM
Corriedale wool; needle felted
PHOTO BY ARTIST

Jasmine Matus

Felt Vessel Pods for Protection I, II, III | 2008

EACH: 36 X 12 X 12 CM

Merino fleece, alpaca; wet felted, stitched

PHOTO BY ADNAN CHOWDHURY

Julia Ford

Vestiges Series: Seed VI, Planta barbula | 2006

16 X 8.5 X 4 CM

Bluefaced Leicester wool; felted

PHOTO BY SCOTT MCCLAINE

Trish Ramsay

Likeness | 2009

LARGE PANTS: 9.1 X 9.3 X 8.1 M

Domestic fleece, steel; wet felted

PHOTO BY ARTIST

A site-specific installation created at the Stonehouse Residency in California's Sierra Nevada foothills, Likeness was made in response to the rugged landscape and the resourceful Western ethos. It explores both culture and nature. The felted pants reference the labor required by the land but also speak to a biological and spiritual inheritance that's passed from one generation to the next. —TR

Hermine Gold
Zärtliche (Armed So Tenderly) | 2006
EACH PIECE: 14 X 12 X 5 CM
Franconian sheep fleece, woolen thread,
steel; wet felted, dyed, stitched, blocked
PHOTOS BY ARTIST

Kerstin Lindström

Just Waiting | 2001

230 X 30 X 30 CM

Felt, cotton thread, recycling material; appliquéd

PHOTO BY ARTIST

Christine White
Cocoon | 2002
10 X 10 X 50 CM
Merino wool; arashi shibori
PHOTOS BY JOHN POLAK PHOTOGRAPHY

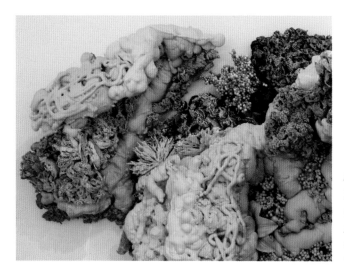

Anneliese Vobis

Biomimicry | 2008

243.8 X 457.2 X 182.9 CM

Acrylic felt, plastic foam, recycled flower
arrangement; knitted, heat treated, cut, structured

PHOTOS BY ARTIST

Lyn Pflueger

feltskin | 2009

153 X 26 CM

Merino and Corriedale fleece, qiviut down and hair, possum, yak, and silk fibers; dyed, wet felted, shibori, re-felted

PHOTO BY MACKENZIE FRERE

Marylena Corrado Sevigney

Deep | 2008

8.8 X 1.5 M

Merino fleece; wet felted, acid dyed

PHOTO BY KAREN PHILIPPI

Sandra Adams

What Goes Around Comes Around | 2009

DIMENSIONS VARY

Merino, Finn, and Romney wools, Shetland fleece, wire,
jute cord, linen, moss, mixed thread, copper wire; wet felted

PHOTO BY ARTIST

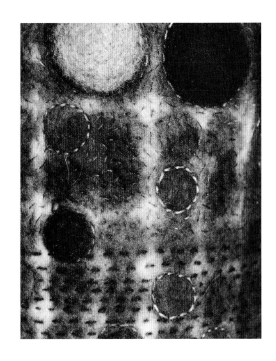

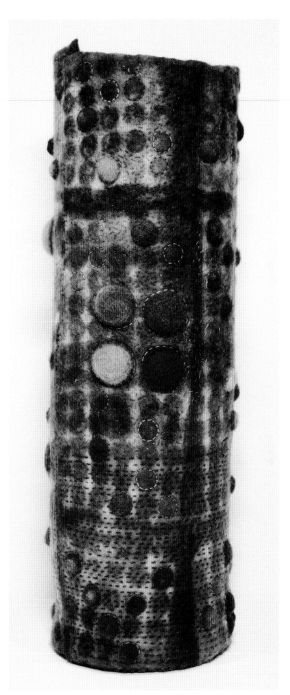

Marty Jonas
Bubble Wrap | 2010
39.3 X 13 X 13 CM
Merino pre-felt, cotton and silk threads; acid
dyed, shibori, hand embroidered, needle felted
PHOTOS BY JOHN M. JONAS

Susan Mills

Copper Elemental | 2008

22.9 X 15.2 X 10.2 CM

Merino fleece, llama fleece, silk, stone, copper; wet felted, dyed, stitched

PHOTO BY CHARLIE LEMAY

Miek Vlamings
Seven Days a Week | 2003
RIGHT: 30 X 44 X 12 CM; LEFT: 46 X 42 X 12 CM
Felt, glass, gold, wax; shibori
PHOTO BY ARTIST

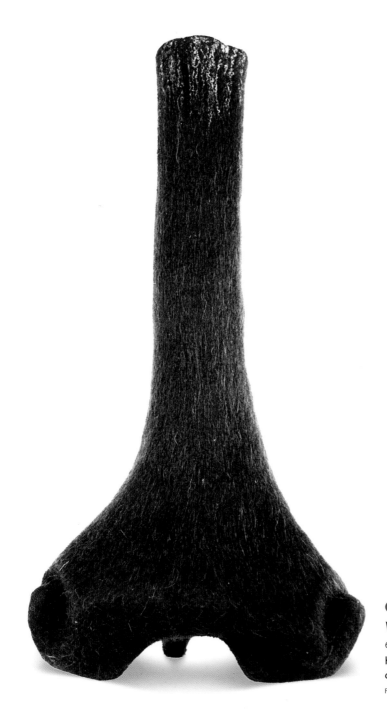

Csilla Wenczel
Vessel Object | 2010
60 X 30 X 30 CM
Karakul sheep fleece, silk;
dyed, wet felted, brushed
PHOTO BY ARTIST

Carol Ingram

Meshomasic Extrusion | 2008

48.3 CM TALL

Merino roving, silk, wire, wool yarn, glass beads, cotton
thread; wet felted, assembled, stitched, coil wrapped

PHOTOS BY JODY BREWER

Lisa Klakulak
Electric Water | 2009
21.6 X 25.4 X 15.2 CM
Merino wool fleece, cotton, metallic thread, waxed linen thread; wet felted, hand stitched, embellished, constructed, steam blocked
PHOTO BY STEVE MANN

Robyn A. Daniel
Interior Language | 2008
29.2 X 42.6 X 7 CM
Merino wool; wet felted, carved, sewn
PHOTO BY ARTIST

Maris Herr
Angel Book 2 | 2008
CLOSED: 24 X 7 X 7 CM; OPEN: 24 X 177 CM
Merino fleece, ash, feathers, silk thread, glass
beads; wet felted, hand stitched, embroidered
PHOTOS BY ARTIST

Angelika Werth
Ode to the RCMP | 2007
SIZE 6
Merino wool, silk, deconstructed
wool blanket fibers, fishhooks; hand
felted, stitched, constructed
PHOTO BY JEREMY ADDINGTON

Denise Richard

Florine | 2008

24 X 45 X 105 CM

Merino fleece, reed; wet felted, woven

PHOTO BY JEFF CRAWFORD

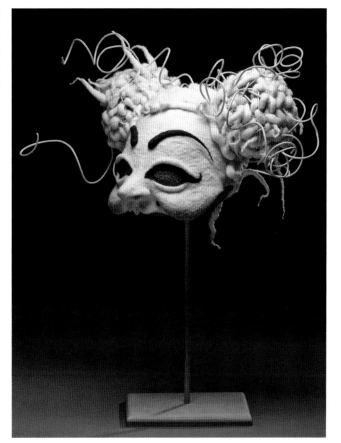

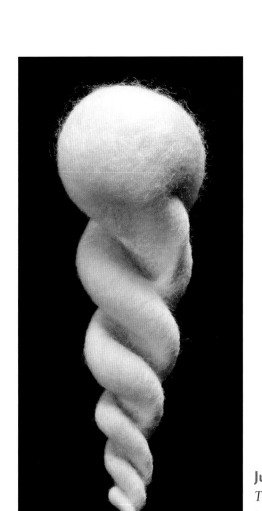

Julia Ford

Twist Series: Helix, Circumvolvo | 2009

24 X 7.5 X 7.5 CM

Coopworth and Australian wools; felted

PHOTO BY SCOTT MCCLAINE

Roza Makashova
Kyrgyz Balls | 2009
LARGEST: 45 X 45 X 45 CM
Wool fleece; wet felted
PHOTO BY EVGENIY SYCHEV

Ieva Krumina
A Piece of Cosmic Dust | 2008
18 X 18 X 18 CM
Merino fleece, polyethylene; wet felted,
needle felted, stitched, embroidered
PHOTO BY OJARS GRIKIS

Vilttoverij sAnNaS
Magnificent Magnetic Effects | 2009
15 X 45 X 45 CM
Merino fleece, synthetic organza, magnets;
dyed, wet felted, nuno techniques
PHOTOS BY KAREN VISSER

Samantha Skelton

Insulate | 2009

10 X 16 X 16 CM

Alpaca fleece, sterling silver; wet
felted, stretched, planished

PHOTO BY JEFF SABO

Cory Phillips

Blue Moon Bowl | 2009

22 X 22 X 10 CM

Wool; dyed with carrot tops, wet felted, cut

PHOTO BY ARTIST

Sonya Yong James
Anthropod | 2009
38 X 66 CM
Coopworth wool roving, dyed merino
wool roving; knitted, shibori, wet felted
PHOTOS BY LOUIS CAHILL

Claire A. Baker

One Shoe | 2009

11 X 8.5 X 2.5 CM

Merino wool, found papers, vintage
photograph, recycled felt, old button; hand
felted with resist, machine embroidered

PHOTOS BY TIM ADAMS

Martine House

Iceless? | 2009

CLOSED: 29.7 X 22.7 X 22.7 CM; OPEN: 27.3 X 62 X 62 CM

Wool roving, wool fabric, cotton and silk fabrics,
embroidery threads, stones, copper; needle
felted, hand embroidered, embellished

PHOTOS BY STEWART STOKES

Marjolein Dallinga
Red Craters | 2009
65 X 60 X 3 CM
Merino wool; partially hand dyed, wet felted
PHOTO BY ARTIST

Anna Kristina Goransson

Don't Step on Living Things | 2008

5 X 120 X 300 CM

Merino wool fleece; wet felted, dyed

PHOTOS BY ARTIST

Monica Blattmann

Metamorphosis | 2009

DIMENSIONS VARY

Merino fleece; wet felted, hand felted

PHOTO BY ARTIST

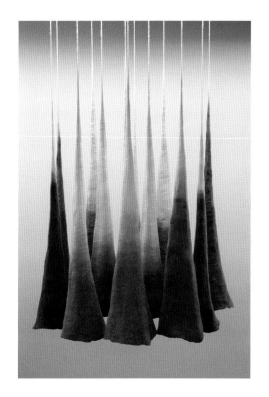

Anna Kristina Goransson
Sanctuary | 2008
210 X 215 X 240 CM
Merino wool fleece; wet felted, dyed
PHOTOS BY ARTIST

Alissa Friedman

Progression | 2009

LARGEST: 38.1 X 38.1 X 38.1 CM

Glass, foam, glue; wet felted, dyed

PHOTOS BY AMANDA LOWE

Yvonne Wakabayashi
Cut Lace Wool Jellyfish Installation | 2009
DIMENSIONS NOT AVAILABLE
Single-knit wool; cut, shibori, wet felted, formed
PHOTO BY KENJI NAGAI

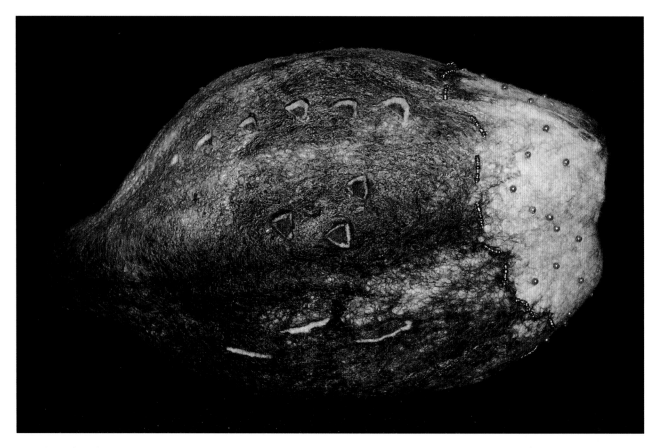

Cindy Obuck

Coco Pod—Large | 2009

12.7 X 27.9 X 20.3 CM

Silk, merino wool, foam piping, beads;
wet felted, hand carved, hand stitched

PHOTO BY ARTIST

Jacqueline Bourque
Volcano | 2009
11.2 X 22 X 18.5 CM
Merino fleece, glass beads; dyed, wet felted, beaded
PHOTO BY DREW GILBERT

Angelika Werth

From the Madeleines Series: Fencing Dress for Joséphine Bonaparte | 2010

SIZE 6

Wool, silk, silver fringe, épée, fencing mask; hand felted, hand embroidered, constructed, stitched

PHOTO BY JEREMY ADDINGTON

Brigitte Haldemann

Bicheno Beach | 2009

39 X 24 X 24 CM

Australian merino fleece, Corriedale wool, shells, silk fabrics, silk fibers, wool thread; wet felted, resist techniques, hand shaped

PHOTO BY PETER VORLICEK

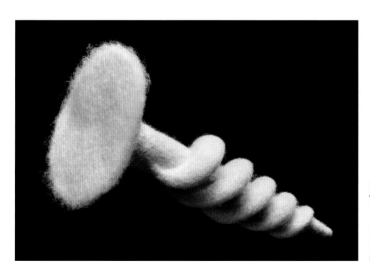

Julia Ford

Twist Series: Screw, Dum spiro, spero | 2009

24 X 11.5 X 11.5 CM

Bluefaced Leicester wool; felted

PHOTO BY SCOTT MCCLAINE

Pamela A. MacGregor

Devil's Claw | 2009

30.5 X 16.5 X 16.5 CM

Merino fleece, devil's claw pod; wet felted

PHOTO BY ARTIST

Elizabeth Finger

Gift from Ghana | 2008

22 X 25 X 25 CM

Harrisville wool, beads; wet felted, sculpted

PHOTO BY RICK WELLS

311

Roza Makashova

Floor Covering: Commercial Break | 2009

10 X 70 X 140 CM

Wool fleece; wet felted

PHOTO BY EVGENIY SYCHEV

Gunilla Paetau Sjöberg

*Dark Room Installation: Anima and Mater
Dolorosa* | 1987

ANIMA (LEFT): 265 CM HIGH; MATER DOLOROSA (RIGHT): 230 CM HIGH

Swedish fine wool, Rya wool, natural colors; wet felted

PHOTO BY GUNNAR HENRIKSSON

These bowls were made from square pieces of industrial felt. I sewed the corners of each piece together, then turned each one inside out, which resulted in a floral shape. I dyed the small bowl red using cherry Kool-Aid. —PHWS

Pamela H.W. Sager
None | 2009
LEFT: 2 X 14 CM; RIGHT: 6.4 X 14 CM
Industrial felt; dyed, stitched
PHOTOS BY ARTIST

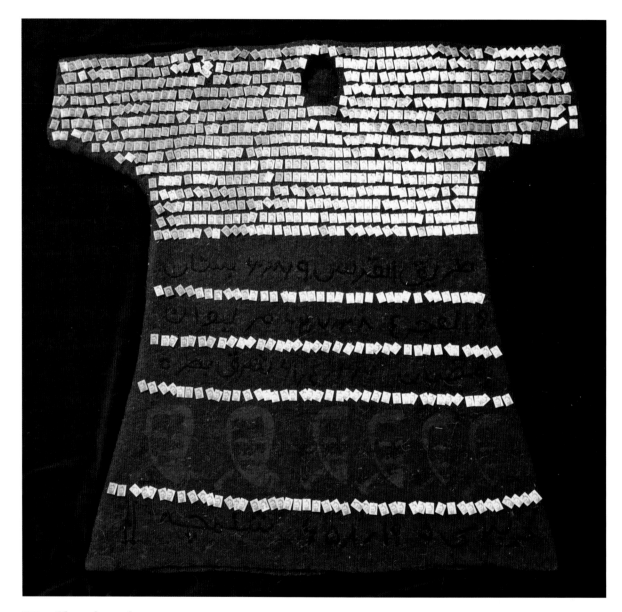

Bita Ghezelayagh
Felt Memories III | 2009
102 X 116 CM
Metal prints, felt; embroidered, silk-screened
PHOTO BY ARTIST

Annie Pennington
Ligand | 2009
14 X 11.4 X 5.1 CM
Merino fleece, rayon flock, copper, brass,
steel; hand sculpted, wet felted, fabricated
PHOTO BY ARTIST

315

Stephanie Metz
Super Suckler | 2008
32 X 38 X 84 CM
Corriedale wool; needle felted
PHOTO BY ARTIST

Tricia A. Stackle
Study of White Forms: Wrapped and Revealing | 2009

LARGEST: 25 CM

Merino fleece, silk thread, ceramic and plastic figurines; wet felted, stitched

PHOTOS BY ARTIST

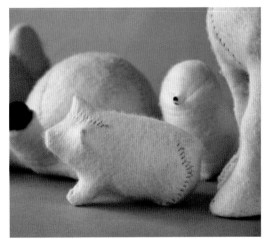

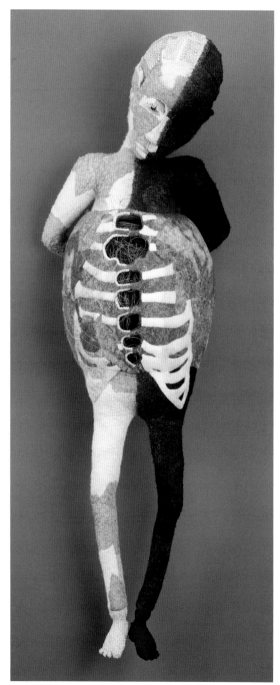

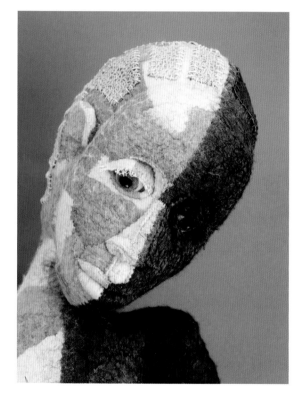

Lisa Klakulak
Internal Chaos | 2009

88.9 X 43.2 X 17.8 CM

Merino wool fleece, silk, tulle, reclaimed wire, avocado and cantaloupe skin, cotton and waxed linen thread, glass seed beads, cotton fill; dyed, wet felted, hand stitched, beaded

PHOTOS BY STEVE MANN

Stephanie Metz
Teddy Skull: Ursulus disneyus solicitudo | 2008
15.3 X 12.8 X 15.3 CM
Corriedale wool; needle felted
PHOTOS BY ARTIST

Anna Gunnasdòttir
Glow | 2010
30 X 60 CM
Icelandic wool, silver wire, handmade silver pearls; hand felted
PHOTO BY FINNBOGI MARINOSSON

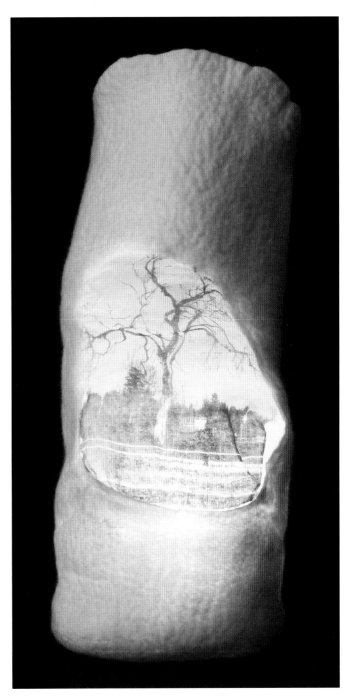

Monica Lacey
Remember Summer | 2010
36.8 CM TALL
Merino fleece, silk organza, candle;
wet felted, screen-printed
PHOTOS BY ARTIST

Emily Wohlscheid

Geodes | 2007

64 X 55 X 8 CM

Merino wool, glass beads, beading
thread; wet felted, beaded, sewn

PHOTO BY BRIAN STEELE

Andrew Kline
Tricia Stackle

Nest: Pink | 2009

DIMENSIONS VARY

Merino fleece, domestic blended fleece,
bungee cords, silk; acid dyed, wet felted, nuno techniques

PHOTO BY ARTISTS

Linda Brooks Hirschman
Lilium Serpentine | 2010
66 X 66 X 69 CM
Merino fleece, commercial fabric,
wire, copper extension rod, yarn; wet
felted, shaped, stiffened, assembled
PHOTOS BY PETER JACOBS

Monica Blattmann
Green Silk Scarf | 2009
200 X 50 X 0.2 CM
Silk chiffon, silk, merino; hand
felted, nuno techniques, wet felted
PHOTO BY ARTIST

Chiu-Tzu-Ying
Spread | 2009
COVER: 30 X 25 X 20 CM; CUP PADS: 18 X 12 CM EACH
Merino fleece; wet felted
PHOTO BY ARTIST

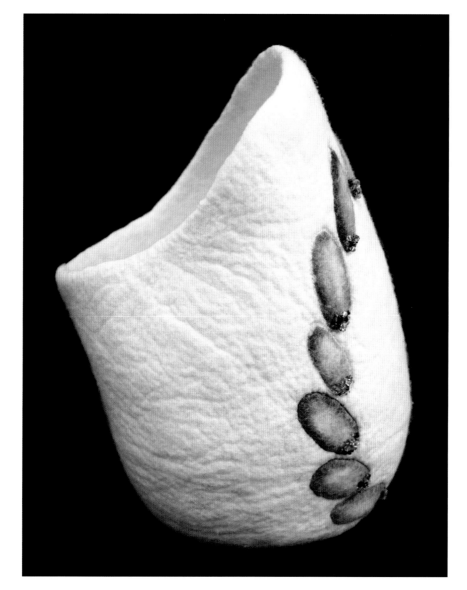

Marty Jonas
Ashes | 2009
22.8 X 15.2 X 16.5 CM
Merino wool roving, merino/cultivated silk roving, silk
thread, assorted beads; wet felted, dyed, stitched
PHOTO BY JOHN M. JONAS

Tanya Aguiniga
Soft Rocks | 2010
LARGEST: 61 X 61 X 127 CM
Norwegian C-1/ Pelsull wool blend, wool,
goat, cow, and camel yarns, upholstery
foam scraps; wet felted
PHOTO BY DAVID SAN MIGUEL

Jacqueline Bourque
Buoy | 2009
9.5 X 13 X 10.5 CM
Merino fleece, silk roving, waxed linen thread,
glass beads; wet felted, knotless netting
PHOTO BY DREW GILBERT

Kerstin Lindström
The Collectors | 2007
EACH: 100 X 70 X 70 CM
Felt, synthetic stuffing; dyed, plissé
PHOTO BY ARTIST

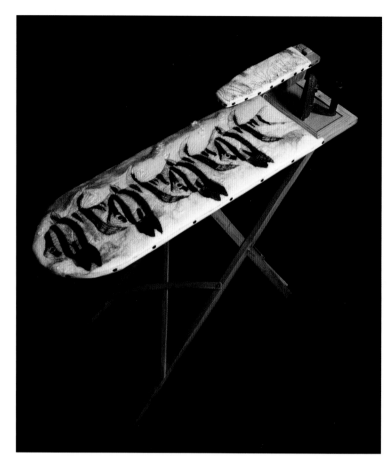

Sandra Tredwell

Something Fishy on Grandma's Ironing Board | 2005

100 X 110 X 30 CM

Antique ironing board, Australian merino tops, silk tops, embroidery thread; wet felted, inlay technique, machine embroidered

PHOTOS BY MALCOLM DOWNES

Caroline Kelley
Ruffle Vase #1 | 2007

46.2 X 20.4 X 20.4 CM

Merino yarn, found glass vase, cotton
thread; knitted, wet felted, blocked, trimmed

PHOTO BY DAVID KELLEY

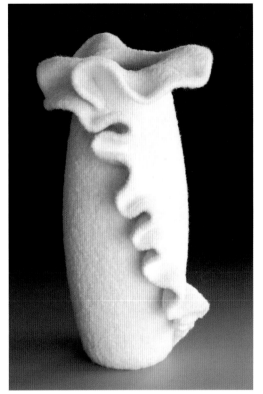

Cory Phillips
Untitled | 2008

73 X 50 X 23 CM

Wool, steel; welded, wet felted, needle felted

PHOTO BY ARTIST

Lily Liu
Soft Vessel | 2006
12.7 X 10.2 X 33 CM
Merino fleece; dyed, wet felted
PHOTO BY JOHN HASEGAWA

Genevieve Packer
Home Security Blind | 2008
160 X 90 X 0.3 CM
Industrial wool felt; hand punched,
trimmed, mounted
PHOTOS BY ARTIST

Yvonne Habbe

Unknown seeds | 2005

EACH PIECE: 150 X 25 CM

Swedish fine wool; wet felted

PHOTOS BY ARTIST

Gunilla Paetau Sjöberg

Place of Fire Installation: Flake of Soot and Flake of Sorrow | 2000

EACH: 260 X 60 CM

Swedish fine wool, flax, silk and mohair fibers, linen, cotton and wool thread, steel wire; dyed, wet felted

PHOTO BY JAN STORM

Anna Kristina Goransson
Vesicle | 2009
150 X 305 X 7 CM
Merino wool fleece; wet felted, dyed
PHOTO BY ARTIST

Sylvia Kind
Wool Wrap Stone | 2009
LARGEST PIECE: 70 X 110 X 90 CM
Merino fleece, grass seed, grass; wet felted
PHOTO BY ARTIST

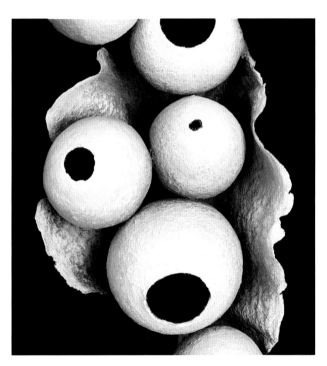

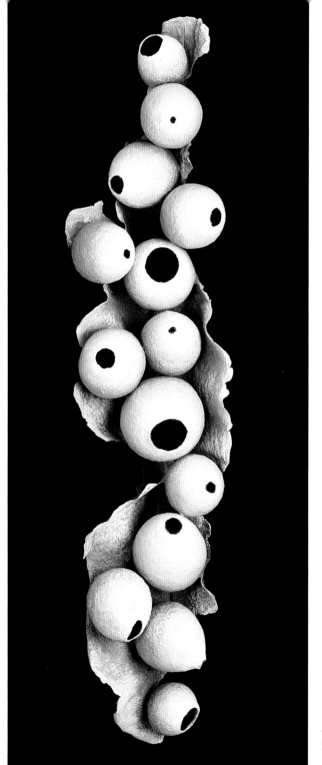

Beth Beede

Heart of Darkness | 2008

119.4 X 27.9 X 27.9 CM

Merino fleece, papier-mâché; wet felted

PHOTOS BY JOHN POLAK

Anna Gunnasdòttir

Birth | 2007

180 X 120 CM

Icelandic wool, copper wire, stones; hand felted

PHOTO BY FINNBOGI MARINOSSON

Vilttoverij sAnNaS
The Magic Basin | 2006
40 X 30 X 20 CM
Merino fleece, raw fleece, mountain sheep wool; wet felted
PHOTO BY ANS VAN DEN BELD

Linda C. Golden
Fetish Bundle from the Found Series: Tops | 2010
3.7 X 2.8 X 0.8 CM
Wool roving, cotton, wire, found bottle
tops, thread; wet felted, hand dyed, clamp
technique, stitched, assembled, wrapped
PHOTO BY ARTIST

Miek Vlamings
Nieuwe Steek van de Prins | 2003
120 X 44 X 3 CM
Wool felt; handmade
PHOTO BY ARTIST

Gil Leitersdorf

Architectural E-Cut Version of a Tulip | 2009

80 X 90 X 90 CM

Merino wool, alpaca, Bluefaced Leicester fleece, camel hair,
massam tops, white tussah silk; handmade, wet felted, folded, cut

PHOTOS BY RAN ERDA

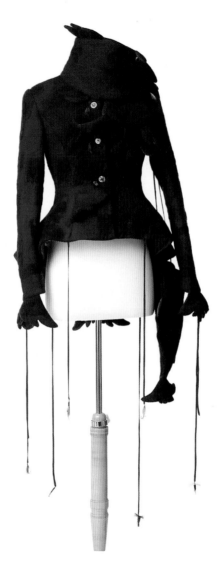

Angelika Werth

Ode to the Fishmonger | 2007

SIZE 6

Merino wool, silk, deconstructed wool
blanket fibers, vintage buttons; hand
felted, stitched, constructed

PHOTO BY JEREMY ADDINGTON

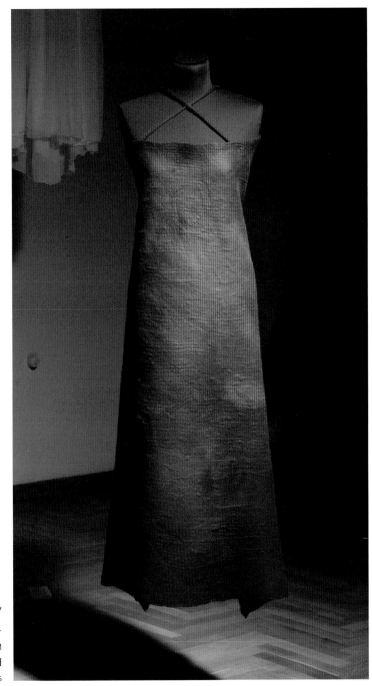

Mari Nagy
Desert Women | 2004
170 X 45 CM
Merino fleece; dyed
PHOTO BY ÀGH ANDRAS

Inge Lindqvist

Topograms | 2001

FOREGROUND: 180 X 180 X 90 CM; LEFT: 180 X 160 CM; RIGHT: 150 X 180 CM

Industrial felt, lamb's wool; wet felted, steamed, shaped

PHOTO BY BENT RYBERG

Janice Arnold
Chroma Passage | 2010
10.4 X 2.4 X 15.2 M
Wool, silk, cotton, bamboo, lyocell, rayon,
Soysilk, mohair, metal; hand felted
PHOTO BY TIM MOTLEY

Cheryl Krismer

Lady Pink Filigree | 2010

96 X 50 X 55 CM

Boiled wool, merino fleece, industrial felt,
vintage chair; wet felted, stitched, upholstered

PHOTOS BY CHRISTOPHER LAWSON

Yvonne Laurysen and Erik Mantel for Lama Concept

Felt Net Screen | 2007

210 X 70 CM

100% virgin wool felt, aluminum frame; punched

PHOTO COURTESY OF LAMA CONCEPT

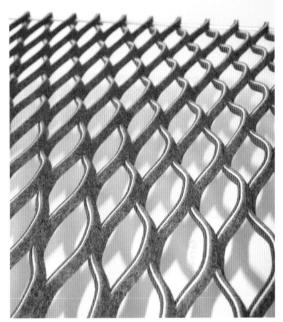

Farha Dharshi

Helix Print Blanket, Grafik Print Rug, Sky Print Pillows, Smoke Print Pillows | 2008

DIMENSIONS VARY

Merino fleece, feather insert, Corriedale wool; wet felted, hand spun, needle felted, stitched

PHOTO BY MELISSA CAMPBELL

Jennifer Anderson

Drove | 2006

EACH: 53 X 51 X 51 CM

Walnut, plastic, industrial felt; cut,
adhered, folded, glued, attached

PHOTO BY LARRY STANLEY

Aurelie Tu
Large Pendant Light | 2010
129.5 X 129.5 CM
100% industrial wool felt; water-jet cut
PHOTO BY LINCOLN BARBOUR PHOTOGRAPHY

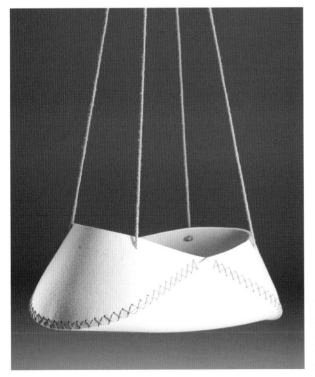

Søren Ulrick Petersen
Swing Low Cradle | 1997
80 X 35 X 22 CM
Wool felt, hemp rope
PHOTO BY ARTIST

Ona Yopack

Green Trusses Curtain | 2009

327.7 X 101.6 CM

Merino pre-felt, silk organza; wet felted, nuno techniques

PHOTOS BY JACKIE MATHEY

Jorie Johnson

Autumn Walk Series: Gourds I & II | 2008

DIMENSIONS VARY

Swiss Walliser fleece, flax, vegetable, chemical, and natural dyes, raw tussah silk floss, kudzu fiber, skeletal leaves; hand felted

PHOTO BY YUZO TOYODA

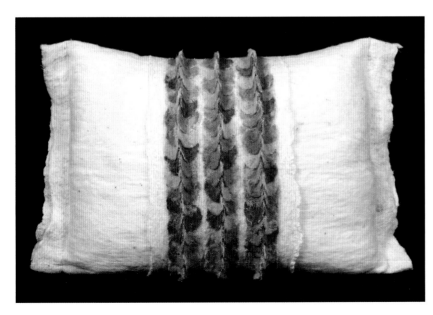

Jamie Galloway

Lean on Me Pillow | 2010

28 X 43 X 10 CM

Organic cotton, merino wool, organic cheesecloth, recycled pillow form; nuno techniques, needle felted, machine stitched

PHOTO BY ARTIST

furnish

Shadow Coaster | 2006

0.2 CM THICK

Polyester and rayon felt

PHOTO BY JUNYA SAKAGUCHI

furnish

Bottle Vases | 2008

TALLEST: 25.5 X 19.5 CM

Ethylene vinyl acetate

PHOTO BY JUNYA SAKAGUCHI

Gräf & Lantz

Cameo Wine Carriers | 2008

EACH: 40.6 X 8.9 X 8.9 CM

Merino felt, vegetable-tanned leather

PHOTO BY ARTIST

Monika Piatkowski for Hive
Circulation Rug/Wall Hanging | 2001
SIZES MADE TO COMMISSION
Wool felt pellets, hessian, latex
PHOTOS COURTESY OF HIVE

Koko Architecture + Design
Leftovers Rug | 2009
70 X 260 X 3 CM
Recycled industrial felt
PHOTOS BY GRACE HUANG

Nicole Chazaud Telaar

Spiral Chair | 2004

96.5 X 81.3 X 81.3 CM

Proprietary blend wool fiber, acid dye, chair;
wet felted, hand painted, upholstered

UPHOLSTERED BY DEBBIE FISHER
PHOTO BY DEAN POWELL

Lene Frantzen
Seat Slice Seat cushion | 2004
38 CM IN DIAMETER
Wool; wet felted
PHOTOS BY THOMAS GUNGE

Boys Table *uses stacked felt as a practical solution to space constraints. By allowing the felt to be reconfigured at varying heights, the table has a flexibility that reflects the material choice.* —KA

Koko Architecture + Design
Boys Table | 2001
90 X 120 X 30 CM
Industrial felt; die cut
PHOTOS BY STEWART FEREBEE

Ben K. Mickus
Floor Perch | 2008
41 X 48 X 86 CM
Natural wool felt, aluminum,
non-toxic adhesives; water-jet cut, welded
PHOTO BY ROBERT BEAN

Stephanie Odegard
Felt Stitched Geometric | 2009
AVAILABLE IN STANDARD AND COMMISSIONED SIZES
Wool felt, cotton embroidery;
hand felted, embroidered
PHOTO BY ODEGARD INC.

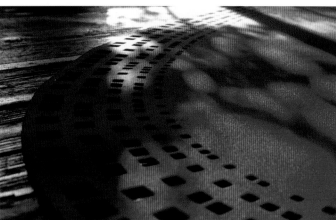

Alfredo Häberli

Salim | 2005

160 X 320 CM

Pure new wool; felted

PHOTOS COURTESY OF RUCKSTUHL

Katharina Wahl

JU87-G STUKA | 2007

40 X 300 X 200 CM

Colored rubber, synthetic textile;
needle felted, printed, water-cut

PHOTOS BY ARTIST

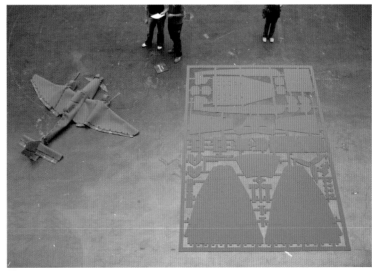

JU87-G STUKA *is a living room-sized model
kit. It features a decorative pattern that's based
on the design of the dreaded German aircraft from
World War II. After four hours of cutting, rolling,
and folding, I was rewarded with a soft JU87-G
STUKA with a three-meter wingspan.* —KW

Stephanie Odegard
Embroidered Felt in White | 2007
AVAILABLE IN STANDARD AND COMMISSIONED SIZES
Wool felt, cotton embroidery; hand felted, embroidered
PHOTO BY JOHN BIGELOW TAYLOR

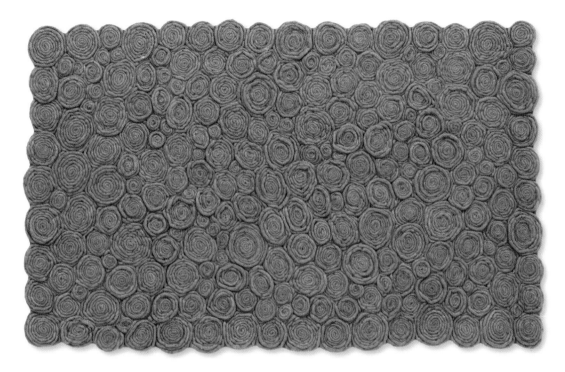

Martín Azú + Gerard Moliné for nanimarquina

Spiral Collection | 2010

SIZES VARY FROM 80 X 140 CM TO 200 X 300 CM

New Zealand wool; handmade, hand sewn, boiled

PHOTOS BY ALBERT FONT

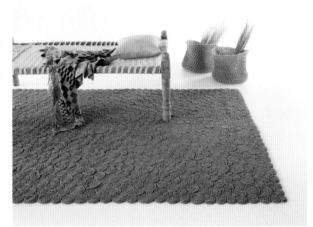

Pudelskern
Morse Table | 2009
40 X 80 X 120 CM
Steel, Tyrolean wool
PHOTOS BY MARKUS BSTIELER

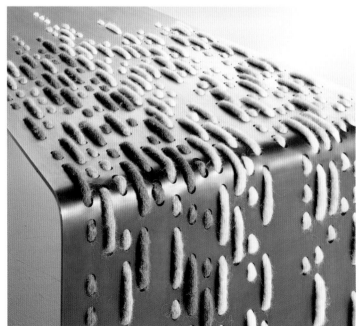

The woolen threads in this table are stitched in a Morse code pattern. It's a simple object with an encrypted secret. —P

cate&nelson
tacto | 2007
38 X 140 X 47 CM
Medium-density fiberboard, birch, metal, wool
PHOTO BY ARTIST

Anne Kyyrö Quinn
Circle Cushion | 2001
60 X 60 CM
Wool felt; sewn
PHOTO BY ARTIST

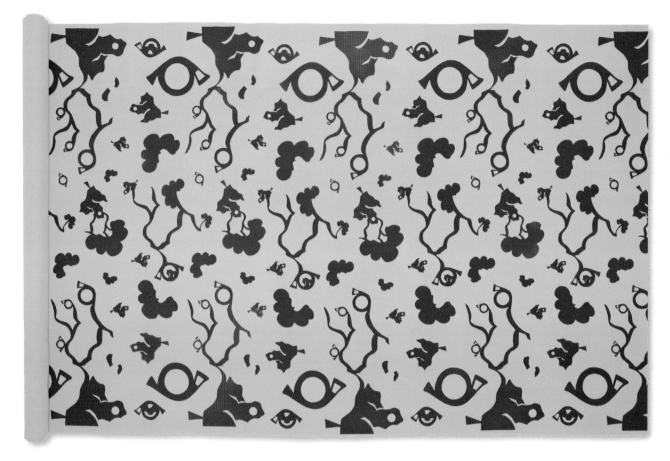

Ineke van der Struijs
Alps Wall Covering | 2005
1.5 X 4 M
Industrial wool felt; screen-printed
PHOTOS BY MARK GROEN

Tanya Aguiniga
Felted Eames DCM | 2008
76 X 45 X 45 CM
Norwegian C-1/Pelsull wool blend,
found steel chair; wet felted
PHOTO BY DAVID SAN MIGUEL

Tanya Aguiniga
Felt Chairs | 2004
EACH: 76 X 45 X 45 CM
Norwegian C-1/Pelsull wool blend,
found steel chairs; wet felted
PHOTO BY DAVID SAN MIGUEL

Kathryn Walter
FELT Molding | 2009
5 X 15.3 CM
Industrial felt
PHOTO BY ARTIST

Moorhead & Moorhead
Felt Stools | 2000
EACH: 43 X 36 X 36 CM
Industrial felt; folded, fastened
PHOTO BY ARTISTS

The Felt Stools *were inspired by, and are the result of, exploring the natural properties of felt.* —M&M

Anne Kyyrö Quinn
Rosette Acoustic Wall Panel
in two color ways | 2006
170 X 300 CM
100% wool felt; sewn
PHOTOS BY 7 GODS, INTERIOR DESIGN

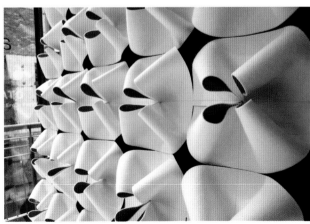

Tom Dixon
Felt Shade Floor Lamps | 2006
EACH: 145 X 70 CM
Felt; double layered, heat pressed
PHOTOS BY ARTIST

Jennifer Anderson
U Stool | 2002
43 X 53 X 36 CM
Plywood, industrial felt; lacquered, pierced
PHOTO BY LARRY STANLEY

Aurelie Tu
Audrey LE Vessels: Large and Medium | 2010
LARGEST: 48.3 X 25.4 CM IN DIAMETER
100% wool felt; water-jet cut, handwoven
PHOTO BY LINCOLN BARBOUR PHOTOGRAPHY

Erica Schlueter
Hut Boxes | 2009
TALLEST: 22 X 8.5 X 8.5 CM
Merino wool fleece, Finn fleece, Leicester
lamb fleece; needle felted, wet felted
PHOTO BY BILL LEMKE

Janet Crowe
Mugmitt | 2009
9 X 18 X 11 CM
Merino fleece; wet felted
PHOTO BY ARTIST

RolloRollo *was an experiment in creating a sculptural piece of furniture that echoed the simplistic, portable design of Mongolian yurts. The felt rolls can be tied together into a transportable bundle.* —TAS

Tricia A. Stackle
RolloRollo | 2009
76.2 X 165.1 X 76.2 CM
Industrial felt, waxed linen thread; stitched
PHOTO BY ARTIST

Pudelskern

Fat Sheep | 2009

400 CM WIDE

Tyrolean wool; hand woven

PHOTO BY MARKUS BSTIELER

Julie Coghlan

Herdy Cushions | 2008

EACH: 60 X 60 CM

Merino fleece, recycled Herdwick
fleece; wet felted, stitched

PHOTO BY ROGER LEE

Grazia Galli
Laura Salvioni
Onda/Wave | 2009
60 X 120 CM
Merino, cotton gauze; nuno techniques
PHOTOS BY DAVIDE CERATI

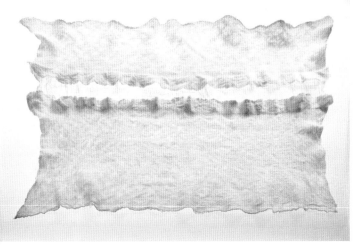

Gräf & Lantz
Felt Bowl | 2009
34.2 CM IN DIAMETER
Merino felt
PHOTOS BY ARTIST

Kathryn Walter
FELT Quilt #2 | 2009
182.9 X 149.9 CM
Industrial wool felt remnants, cotton backing; machine stitched
PHOTO BY DIANA BRAUN-WOODBURY

Julia Romanova

Ohm | 2008

60 X 180 CM

Merino fleece; wet felted, embroidered, nuno techniques

PHOTO BY ARTIST

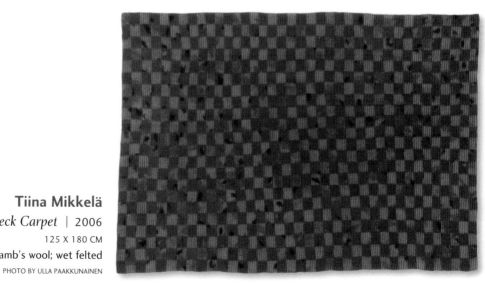

Tiina Mikkelä

Check Carpet | 2006

125 X 180 CM

Finnish lamb's wool; wet felted

PHOTO BY ULLA PAAKKUNAINEN

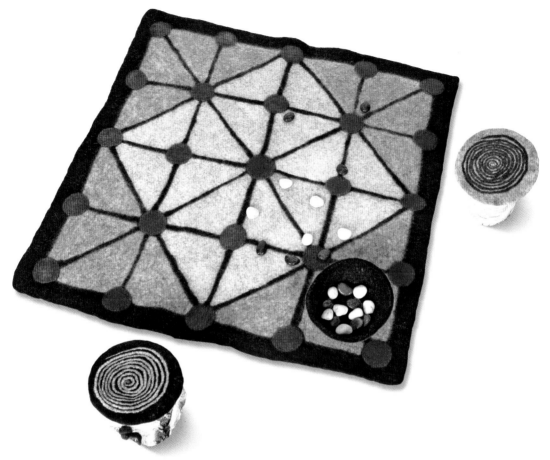

Uta Marschmann
Play Carpet Ensemble: Alquerque | 2007
110 X 110 CM
Mountain sheep fleece, birch, pebbles; wet felted
PHOTOS BY ALEXANDER HEUBERGER

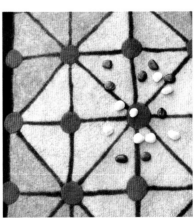

Gill Ferguson

Flower Ring | 2008

110 X 150 X 2 CM

Norwegian fleece; wet felted, laser cut

PHOTO BY ARTIST

Grazia Galli
Laura Salvioni

Albero/Tree | 2009

EACH SECTION: 50 X 320 CM

Carded wool; wet felted

PHOTO BY DAVIDE CERATI

Rosemary Mifsud
Felt Rug | 2008
121.9 X 213.4 X 1.3 CM
Carpet-grade felt, wool, latex; hand
cut, laminated, sewn, embroidered
PHOTOS BY PIETER VANTUYL

Sharon Costello

Skins #1 | 2008

53.3 X 43.2 X 35.6 CM

Merino wool, wool nubs, cotton cheesecloth, flax, willow, recycled lampshade framework, light fixture; seamless felted

PHOTO BY JOHN ARRIGHI

Claudio Varone
Anneke Copier

Le Ostriche | 2010

160 CM LONG

Wool; wet felted

PHOTO BY ARTISTS

Ayala Serfaty
Apaya | 2009
EACH COLUMN: 178 CM TALL
Merino fleece, mohair; wet felted

COLLABORATION WITH IRIT DULMAN
PHOTOS BY ALBI SERFATY

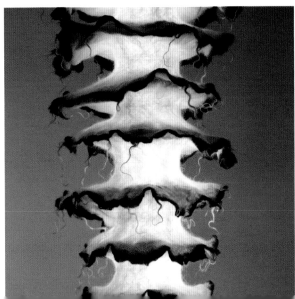

furnish

Felt Placemats | 2006

EACH: 27 X 39 X 0.2 CM

Polyester felt

PHOTOS BY JUNYA SAKAGUCHI

Chiara Cibin

Diogene | 2000

200 X 100 X 50 CM

Industrial felt, industrial plywood
structure; handmade, embroidered

PHOTO BY ARTIST

Each Yak Tea Cozy is designed to keep
the handle of a teacup cool while the
liquid inside remains warm. The tea cozy
completely covers a cup, while the cup's
handle peeks out of an opening in the
cozy. The Coffee Cozies are designed for
coffeepots and serve the same purpose. —IL

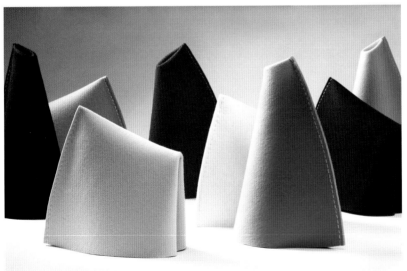

Inge Lindqvist

Yak Tea and Coffee Cozies | 2006

EACH TEA COZY: 30 X 30 X 20 CM;
EACH COFFEE COZY: 40 X 25 X 20 CM

Industrial felt; stitched

PHOTO BY OLE AKHØG

Pierre Sindre
Button I Armchair | 2009
78 X 57 X 52 CM
Ash wood, industrial felt; molded
PHOTO BY LENNART DUREHED

Andrew Kline
Rockin' Chair | 2009
61 X 45 X 56 CM
Birch, industrial felt
PHOTO BY ARTIST

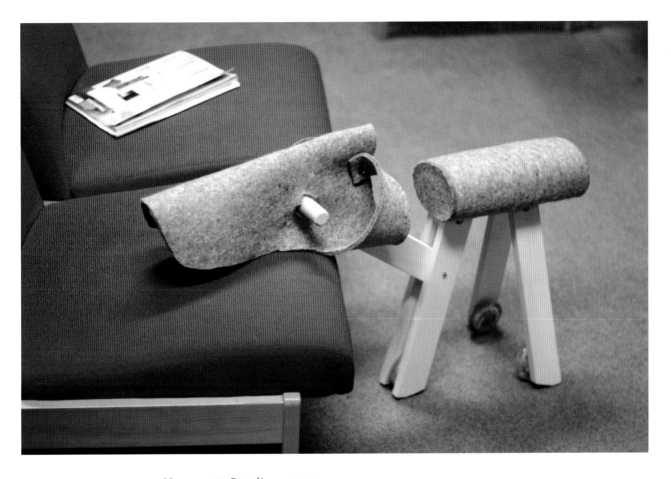

Kompott Studio
(s.o.o.n.) something out of nothing | 2009
33 X 50 X 10 CM
Industrial felt, wood
PHOTOS BY EWA AXELRAD

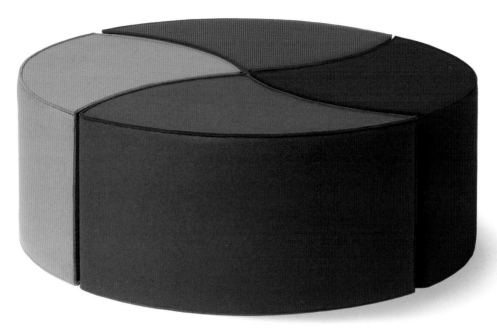

HEY-SIGN

Seat Cushion Posito | 2003

40 X 110 CM

Pure new wool industrial felt,
foam padding; stitched, filled

DESIGNED BY SUSANNE MEIER
PHOTOS BY REIMUND BRAUN

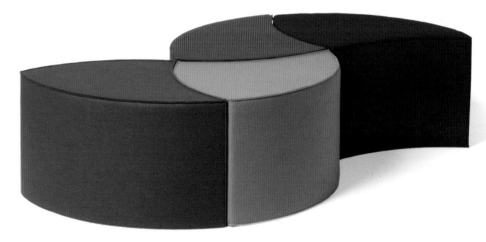

Posito *was inspired by a desire to create flexible seating solutions. The four elements of the piece can be combined in different ways to form new seating arrangements. With felt, the running direction of the fabric isn't a concern, so the different combinations are easy to do and beautiful.* —H-S

Nicole Chazaud Telaar

Like Bees to Honey Sofa | 2005

106.7 X 208.3 X 81.3 CM

Proprietary wool blend, acid dye, antique sofa, upholstery-weight felt; painted, upholstered, wet felted

UPHOLSTERED BY DEBBIE FISHER
PHOTO BY DEAN POWELL

cate&nelson

OZ lowchair | 2007

75 X 70 X 85 CM

Aluminum frame, wool felt

PHOTO BY ARTIST

Irit Dulman
Untitled | 2009
70 X 160 CM
Bergschaf wool, New Zealand wool; wet felted
PHOTO BY ARI AVITS & IDAN LEVY

Gräf & Lantz
Devon Ottoman | 2009
45.7 X 45.7 X 45.7 CM
Merino felt
PHOTO BY ARTIST

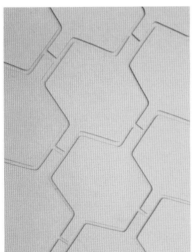

Monika Piatkowski for Hive

Flock Felt Wall Tiles | 2010

25 X 20 CM

Wool felt self-adhesive tiles; die cut

PHOTOS BY RACHAEL SMITH

Ben K. Mickus
Relief Chair | 2009
93 X 81 X 86 CM
Natural wool felt, stainless steel,
non-toxic adhesives; water-jet cut
PHOTO BY ROBERT BEAN

Kathryn Walter
FELT Striation: Screening Room Doors | 2006
240 X 180 X 27 CM
Industrial felt, walnut frames; inlaid
PHOTO BY BJORG MAGNEA

Tom Loeser

Cinch | 2007

EACH UNIT: 46 X 48 X 48 CM

Industrial felt, steel strapping

PUBLIC SEATING INSTALLED IN THE LOBBY OF
THE MADISON MUSEUM OF CONTEMPORARY ART, MADISON, WISCONSIN
PHOTO BY ARTIST

Ataphol Sujirapinyokul

Color Kale | 2008

25 X 50 X 50 CM

Wool, cotton; knitted

PHOTOS BY HENRIK BENGTSSON

Lene Frantzen
Sofa Slice Cushions | 2005
EACH: 35 X 10 CM
Wool, foam; wet felted
PHOTOS BY THOMAS GUNGE

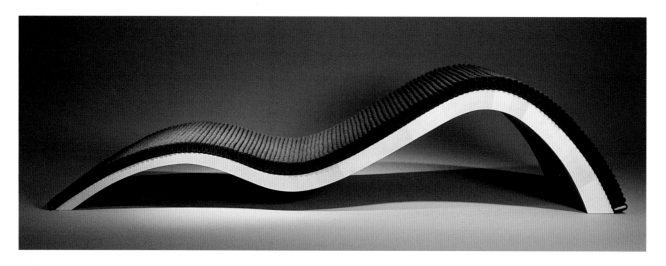

Jennifer Anderson

Echo Chaise | 2004

53 X 66 X 216 CM

Industrial felt, plywood, steel cable; threaded

PHOTOS BY LARRY STANLEY

Anne Kyyrö Quinn
Leaf Panels | 2006
40 X 40 M
Felt; twisted, sewn
PHOTO BY RACHEL JONES

Merja Markkula
November Items | 2007
LARGEST: 55 X 30 X 30 CM
Finn sheep fleece, fabric, willow; wet felted
PHOTO BY ARTIST

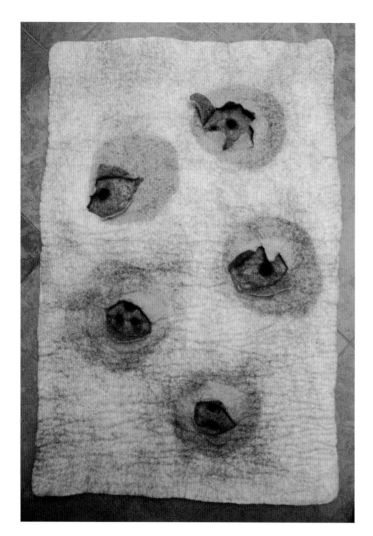

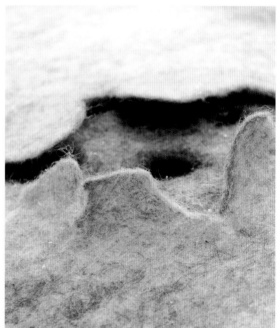

Malin Sjöstrand
Carpet | 2009
100 X 65 X 0.8 CM
Fine wool, Gotland wool; wet felted
PHOTOS BY JACOB PETRÉ

Succulents in the Garden *is a decorative floor, wall, or table covering.* —NS

Nicole Schlesinger
Succulents in the Garden | 2009
43.2 X 76.2 X 1.3 CM
Felt, cotton embroidery floss; laser cut, hand embroidered
PHOTO BY FRAZER SPOWART

Anastasia Bespalova
Field of Bean Sprouts Blanket | 2009
107 X 107 CM
Merino wool, merino and mohair blend; wet felted
PHOTOS BY ARTIST

Cathryn Ward

Bird on Wire throw and cushions | 2009

170 X 115 CM

Merino fleece, muslin, embroidery cotton;
wet felted, nuno techniques, embroidered

PHOTO BY JOLENE CARTMILL

Farha Dharshi

Grafik Print Blanket | 2009

198 X 143 CM

Merino fleece; wet felted

PHOTO BY MELISSA CAMPBELL

Claudy Jongstra
Frisian Wouw | 2010
240 X 330 CM
Pure new wool; felted
PHOTOS COURTESY OF RUCKSTUHL

Katie Mawson

Hedgehog Cushion | 2009

45 X 45 CM

Merino lamb's wool; knitted, felted

PHOTO BY ANDRA NELKI

Elena Kihlman

Rugiada Panel | 2009

270 X 60 X 2 CM

Industrial felt; stitched, crossed

PHOTO BY ELEONORA BLANCO

Toni Pallejà (Porcuatro) for ABR
Feel-Through | 2007
EACH PANEL: 250 X 39 X 1.2 CM
Industrial felt, anodized aluminum
PHOTOS BY ARTIST

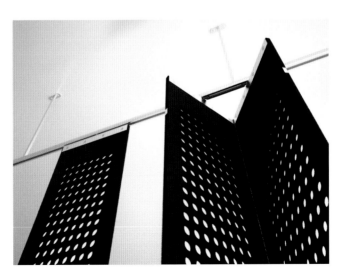

Deborah Moss

Night Sky | 2010

152 CM IN DIAMETER

Pure new wool, dye, crystals;
felted, hand painted, stitched

PHOTOS COURTESY OF RUCKSTUHL

Mauro Vegliante
Riccardo Fattori

SO-UL lightcarpet | 2005

180 CM IN DIAMETER

Industrial felt, clear plastic sheeting

PHOTO BY ARTISTS

Patty Benson
Nesting Bowls: Sunnyside | 2008
LARGEST: 15.2 X 6.4 CM
Wool/mohair yarn; hand crocheted,
wet felted, trimmed, steamed
PHOTO BY ARTIST

Michelle Jarvis
Orange Atoms | 2004
50 X 60 CM
Industrial felt; hand printed, embroidered
PHOTO BY ARTIST

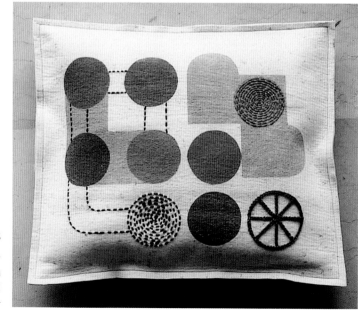

*Felt is similar to clay in that it gives us the
ability to create three-dimensional shapes.
We took advantage of that ability when we made*
Le Terrazze Ardenti. —AC & CV

**Anneke Copier
Claudio Varone**
Le Terrazze Ardenti | 2008
140 X 200 CM
Wool; wet felted
PHOTO BY ARTISTS

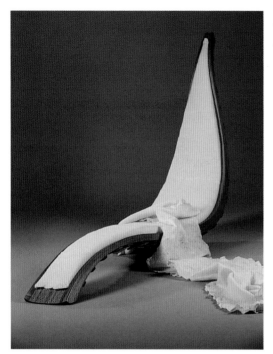

Jennifer Anderson
Chrysalis | 2006
114 X 41 X 216 CM
Mahogany, wool; wet felted, upholstered
PHOTO BY LARRY STANLEY

The Ears Stools *propose innumerable options*
for custom design using multi-layered felt.
They were inspired by the felting process. —AS

Ayala Serfaty
Ears Stools | *2009*
EACH: 45 CM TALL
Bergschaf wool, merino fleece, steel; wet felted
COLLABORATION WITH IRIT DULMAN
PHOTO BY ALBI SERFATY

Bev Hisey

Butterfly Bag Chair and Ottoman | 2010

LARGEST: 152.4 X 45.8 X 114.3 CM

Wool felt, foam; die cut, machine stitched

PHOTO BY DONNA GRIFFITH

Dror

Peacock Chairs | 2009

EACH: 110 X 90 X 43 CM

Wool, metal; varnished

PHOTOS BY CAPPELLINI

I created these chairs without using sewing or upholstery techniques. The sheets of felt are simply folded around metal frames; the tension and the pressure of the folds create each chair's shape. For me, the design represents both physical and metaphorical transformation. —D

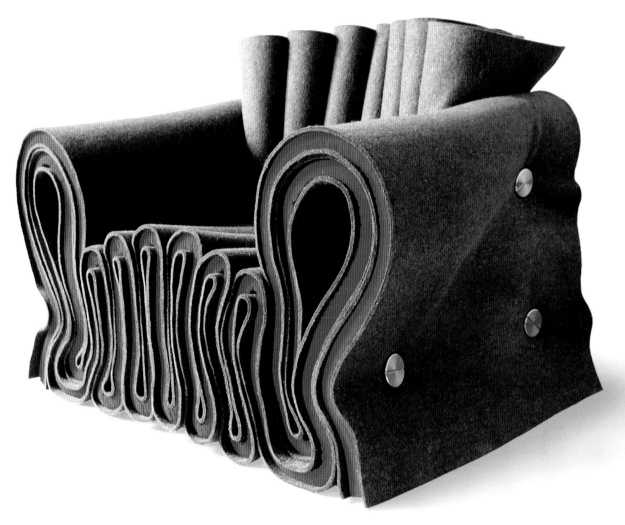

The Joseph Felt Chair *is composed of six rolls of interwoven wool felt pressed together with custom-made stainless-steel fasteners. It's a soft chair that changes through use, like a leather shoe that's broken in over time. It gets personalized through wear.* —LW

Lothar Windels
Joseph Felt Chair | 2000
80 X 110 X 90 CM
Wool felt, stainless steel
PHOTO BY ARTIST

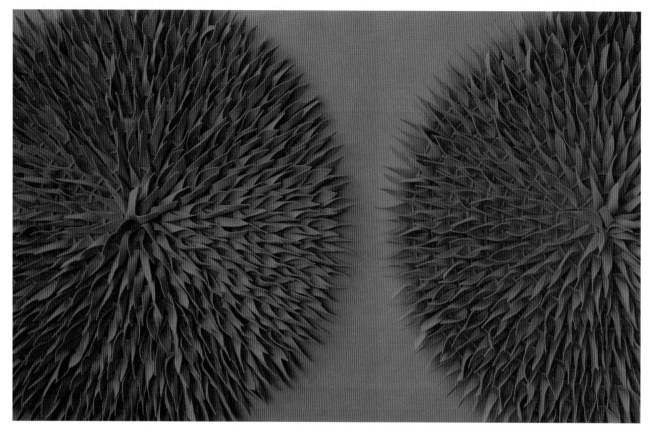

Anne Kyyrö Quinn

Round Tulip Acoustic Wall Panel | 2004

120 X 300 CM

100% wool felt; hand cut, stitched

PHOTO BY LUZELLE VAN DER WESTHUIZEN

Contributing Artists

A

À La Disposition New York, New York 35, 45

Abretti, Tiziana Bologna, Italy 231

Adams, Sandra Indian Head Park, Illinois 284

Aguiniga, Tanya Los Angeles, California 328, 367

Ahern, Sheila Dublin, Ireland 30, 195

Akan, Sezgin Ankara, Turkey 109

Alcorn, Hope Gelfand Pittsburg, Pennsylvania 224, 242

Anderson, Jennifer San Diego, California 348, 371, 396, 410

Andrews, Beth Charlotte, North Carolina 73, 102

Arnold, Janice Centralia, Washington 150, 345

Arvilommi, Karoliina Värtsilä, Finland 32, 239, 252

Asangulova, Nurjamal Bishkek, Kyrgyzstan 206

Åsbjerg, Lone Hornbaek, Denmark 52, 86

Aslett, Katelyn Townsville, Queensland, Australia 18

Auman, Megan Jonestown, Pennsylvania 113

Azú, Martín Barcelona, Spain 363

B

Baker, Claire A. Teesside, England 298

Bath, Maude Adelaide, South Australia, Australia 145

Baumane, Aija Riga, Latvia 219

Beals, Phyllis Santa Rosa, California 97

Beede, Beth Northampton, Massachusetts 337

Begiç H. Nurgül Konya, Turkey 222

Bekic, Lilyana San Diego, California 106, 211

Belcher, Heather London, England 227, 254

Benner, Ulrieke Salt Spring Island, British Columbia, Canada 14, 65, 98

Benson, Patty Alameda, California 408

Berthon, Elisabeth (for Lola Bastille-Paris) La Mulatiere, France 82

Bespalova, Anastasia Modesto, California 85, 400

Binder, Dagmar Berlin, Germany 125, 179, 256

Blattmann, Monica Mettmenstetten, Switzerland 302, 325

Bogdaniene, Egle Ganda Vilnius, Lithuania 237

Bourque, Jacqueline Fredericton, New Brunswick, Canada 307, 328

Bowman, Susan J. Colorado Springs, Colorado 75

Brooks, Gill Marrickville, New South Wales, Australia 207

Brown, Ali Poole, Dorset, England 226

Buch, Charlotte Kirke Eskilstrup, Denmark 140, 201

Burns, Beth Manteo, North Carolina 163

Burr, Marianne Coupeville, Washington 241, 267

Byström, Teresa Arlington, Washington 55

C

Cacicedo, Jean Williams Berkeley, California 88, 212, 230

Carlsen, Lone Birgitte Hornbaek, Denmark 57

Carter, Miriam Dublin, New Hampshire 34, 75

cate&nelson Eskilstuna, Sweden 365, 389

Chao, Yung-Huei Guan Tien Township, Tainan County, Taiwan 127

Chiu-Tzu-Ying Banqiao City, Taipei County, Taiwan 199, 236

Choi, Rowena Brooklyn, New York 59

Church, Kate Mahone Bay, Nova Scotia 268

Cibin, Chiara Este, Italy 385

Clark, Thea Maplewood, New Jersey 123, 205

Clausen, Jens A. Kautokeino, Norway 191

Clay, Liz Wells, Somerset, England 77, 104, 151

Coble, Katie Baltimore, Maryland 22, 96

Coghlan, Julie Cumbria, England 374

Colella, Jodi Wellesley, Massachusetts 263

Copier, Anneke Hauwert, Netherlands 19, 21, 51, 382, 409

Costello, Sharon Rensselaerville, New York 382

Crites-Moore, Morna Redding, Connecticut 248

Crowe, Janet Geneva, Switzerland 132, 372

Cummins, Jane Macclesfield, Cheshire, England 119

Curfman, Anna-Katherine Seattle, Washington 63, 91, 95, 105

D

Daamen, Brigit Haarlem, Netherlands 202

Dallinga, Marjolein Saint-Sauveur, Quebec, Canada 300

Daniel, Robyn A. Stow, Massachusetts 126, 290

Danielis, Gioia Udine, Italy 49, 89

de Groot, Pam Lawson, New South Wales, Australia 78, 89, 103

About the Juror

Susan Brown is associate curator of textiles at the Cooper-Hewitt, National Design Museum in New York City. Curator of the 2009 Cooper-Hewitt exhibit *Fashioning Felt*, she has written and lectured extensively about the material. Susan also recently co-curated *Quicktake: Rodarte* with Gregory Krum and *Color Moves: Art and Fashion by Sonia Delaunay*, both at the Cooper-Hewitt. She is on the faculty of the School of Art and Design History and Theory at Parsons The New School for Design and lectures regularly at the Institute of Fine Arts at New York University. A former costume designer for theater, opera, and television, she holds an M. A. in Museum Studies: Costume and Textiles from the Fashion Institute of Technology.

Acknowledgments

This was such an exciting book to put together! My deepest appreciation goes to the hundreds of gifted artists from around the world who submitted imagery for consideration. These pages are a testament to their talent and to their willingness to share their work.

I'm grateful to Susan Brown, assistant curator at the Cooper-Hewitt, National Design Museum, for serving as juror for the book. She was an enthusiastic partner in this undertaking and shared her expertise at every step. I value her dedication to this project. It was such a pleasure working together.

I'm indebted to Dawn Dillingham, Abby Haffelt, Julie Hale, and Meagan Shirlen at Lark; their diligent work kept the manuscript and layout processes smoothly on track. Matt Shay did a masterful job of laying out the book. Thanks to proofreader Val Anderson for carefully making sure we got everything right.

Nathalie Mornu

Dagmar Binder
Series of 3D Structured Neckpieces | 2006